HANDBOOK
OF SCRIPTS AND
ALPHABETS

HANDBOOK OF SCRIPTS AND ALPHABETS

BY

GEORGE L. CAMPBELL

LONDON AND NEW YORK

First published 1997
by Routledge
11 New Fetter Lane, London EC4P 4EE

Simultaneously published in the USA and Canada
by Routledge
29 West 35th Street, New York, NY 10001

© 1997 George L. Campbell

Typeset by Florencetype Ltd, Stoodleigh, Devon
Printed and bound in Great Britain by
Redwood Books, Trowbridge, Wilts

British Library Cataloguing in Publication Data
A catalogue record for this book is available from the British Library

Library of Congress Cataloguing in Publication Data
Campbell, George L.
Handbook of scripts and alphabets/George L. Campbell.
1. Writing – Handbooks, manuals, etc. 2. Alphabet – Handbooks,
manuals, etc. I. Title.
P211. C25 1997
411–dc20 96-5765

ISBN 0-415-18344-8 (hbk)
ISBN 0-415-13715-2 (pbk)

CONTENTS

PREFACE

The script tables contained in this handbook originally appeared in the form of an appendix to my book, *Compendium of the World's Languages* (Routledge, 1991), where they provided a natural complement to the text articles describing the languages which now use, or once used, these scripts. If they now appear without the relevant articles, it is because the intrinsic interest of the scripts themselves seems to justify their separate publication. Indeed, over and above their main function – that of providing notational systems for human language – many of the scripts have considerable aesthetic appeal; and at least two of them – Chinese and Arabic – become, in the hands of skilled calligraphers, exquisite art forms.

For this handbook, some of the tables have been slightly amended in order to accommodate additional detail, and most of the commentaries have been rewritten and amplified. One item – the script table and commentary for Epigraphic South Arabian – was not included in the *Compendium*.

Ideally, many more examples of orthography, usage, print styles and calligraphy would be called for, but considerations of cost have ruled this out.

I would like to thank Simon Bell for initiating this project, and for his helpful advice and co-operation at all stages of selection and presentation. I would also like to thank Kate Hopgood for her careful editing of a difficult text.

G.L. Campbell

ARABIC

Arabic is written from right to left in an alphabet of twenty-eight letters, all of which are consonants. The language has six vowels, three short and three long. The three short vowels are fatḥa (*a*), kasra (*i*) and ḍamma (*u*). Fatḥa and ḍamma are written above, and kasra below the line. Thus, with the consonant *b*:

بَ ba   بِ bi   بُ bu

The short vowels are not normally written except in pedagogical texts, and, of course, in the Qur'ān, texts of which are always fully vocalized.

The three consonants alif, wāw and yā' are used in the notation of the three long vowels, *ā, ī, ū*, with their short counterparts, fatḥa, kasra and ḍamma, on the preceding consonant: thus, again with *b*:

بَا bā   بِي bī   بُو bū

Twenty-two of the letters are connected in writing both to the preceding and to the following letter; the relevant initial, medial and final forms are set out in the accompanying table. It will be seen, however, that six letters have no medial form: that is, they cannot be joined to a following letter.

Additional signs used in Arabic script:

(a) *Nunation*. An Arabic noun is either definite or indefinite. For most nouns, indefiniteness is expressed by nunation, i.e. the addition of the ending -*un*, marked as ٌ superscript (in the nominative; the marker changes to ً /-an/ and ٍ /-in/ in the oblique cases). For example:

مَدِينَةٌ *madinatun*   مَدِينَةً *medinatan*   مَدِينَةٍ *madinatin* ('town')

(b) *Sukūn*. The superscript marker ْ over a consonant indicates that that consonant is vowelless: e.g. شَرْق 'East', where rā' is marked by sukūn.

(c) *Hamza.* The marker ٶ indicates the glottal stop. The bearer for initial hamza is always alif, with fatḥa, kasra or ḍamma as required. Medially, hamza may be carried by alif, wāw or yā'; finally, it is placed on the line of script.

(d) *Shadda.* A doubled consonant (geminate) is written as a single consonant with the sign ّ over it. This is called shadda or tashdid. Cf.

كَسَرَ 'he broke'

كَسَّرَ 'he smashed to pieces'

(e) *Madda.* If long alif follows the glottal stop, the hamza sign is dropped, and one alif is written as superscript over a second: آ = /ʔaː/. Madda may occur medially, notably in the word قُرْآنٌ *qur'ānun* 'Qur'ān', 'Koran'. Arabic has no capital letters.

The Arabic script is a derivative of the Nabataean consonantal script, which was used for inscriptions in Petra from the second century BC to the second century AD. The earliest manuscripts of the Qur'ān (eighth to tenth century) are written in a style known as Kufic, i.e. associated with the city of Kūfah in Mesopotamia, though this provenance has been questioned. It is the source of the *maghribī* style, which developed in Spain and which is still used in the Arab states of North Africa.

From the eleventh century onwards, the beautiful flowing cursive style known as *naskhī* was developed and perfected to become the Arabic script *par excellence*. This is the form which underlies most contemporary type-fonts. A somewhat simplified form, known as *ruq'a*, has been used for ordinary purposes of handwriting (as distinct from calligraphy) since the Ottoman period. This utilitarian form does not, however, depart from naskhī in the way that 'grass script' (*căo shū*), for example, distorts Chinese standard characters.

There are several offshoots of naskhī, such as the ornate and exquisite *ta'līq* (or *nasta'liq*), much used for poetry in Persian and Urdu, and dīvānī, the script of the Ottoman Turkish imperial chancellery. The supreme *tour de force* of the dīvānī style is the *tuğra* – the monogram or cipher specifically designed for each Sultan. Nowhere is the curious alchemy of the Arabic script made more manifest than in the tuğra: the jinn of pure formal beauty emerges from the bottle of the script. The frontispiece shows the wondrous emblem created for Süleyman the Magnificent.

The Arabic script is, or has been, used to notate many other languages. Among those which have abandoned Arabic script for Roman are Indonesian (Malay), Hausa, Somali, Sundanese, Swahili and Turkish. Several Caucasian languages, e.g. Chechen, Kabardian, Lak, Avar and

Lezgi, used the Arabic script until, after a short period of experimental romanization, Cyrillic was imposed on them. At present, Arabic is retained for a number of important languages, including Persian, Urdu, Pashto, Baluchi, Kurdish, Lahndā, Kashmiri, Sindhi and Uighur. Since the phonological inventories of these languages differ, in some cases markedly, from that of Arabic, the script has had to be augmented and adapted to meet the new demands made upon it. An extreme case is provided by Sindhi, in which certain Arabic letters have been adapted to denote the six retroflex sounds, six aspirates, four implosives and two nasals found in Sindhi. In both Persian and Sindhi certain Arabic letters are redundant, in that two or more Arabic phonemes are reduced to one sound. Thus in Persian the four letters ذ (Ar. /ð/), ز (Ar. /z/), ض (Ar. /ḍ/), ظ (Ar. /z̧/) are all realized as /z/. Similarly, the three Arabic phonemes /θ/, /s/ and /ṣ/ fuse to give /s/.

THE ARABIC SCRIPT

THE ALPHABET

Transliteration	Final	Medial	Initial	Alone	Name
ā	ل			ا	ʔalif
b	ب	ٮ	ٮ	ب	bāʔ
t	ت	ٮ	ٮ	ت	tāʔ
θ	ث	ٮ	ٮ	ث	θaʔ
ǰ	ج	ج	ج	ج	ǰīm
ħ	ح	ح	ح	ح	ħāʔ
x	خ	خ	خ	خ	xāʔ
d	د			د	dāl
ð	ذ			ذ	ðāl
r	ر			ر	rāʔ
z	ز			ز	zāy
s	س	س	س	س	sīn
š	ش	ش	ش	ش	šīn
ṣ	ص	ص	ص	ص	ṣād
ḍ	ض	ض	ض	ض	ḍād
ṭ	ط	ط	ط	ط	tāʔ
ð̣	ظ	ظ	ظ	ظ	ðaʔ
ʕ	ع	ع	ع	ع	ʕayn
ɣ	غ	غ	غ	غ	ɣayn
f	ف	ف	ف	ف	fāʔ
q	ق	ق	ق	ق	qāf
k	ك	ك	ك	ك	kāf
l	ل	ل	ل	ل	lām

Transliteration	Final	Medial	Initial	Alone	Name
m	م	ـم	مـ	م	mīm
n	ن	ـنـ	نـ	ن	nūn
h	ـه	ـهـ	هـ	ه	hāʔ
w	و			و	wāw
y	ى	ـيـ	يـ	ى	yāʔ

Source: Kaye, A.S. (1987) 'Arabic', in B. Comrie (ed.) *The World's Major Languages*, London, Routledge.

NUMERALS

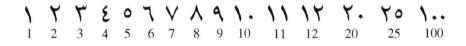

١	٢	٣	٤	٥	٦	٧	٨	٩	١٠	١١	١٢	٢٠	٢٥	١٠٠
1	2	3	4	5	6	7	8	9	10	11	12	20	25	100

ARMENIAN

The thirty-six letters devised early in the fifth century AD by Bishop Mesrop Mashtots to notate the sounds of Classical Armenian have fitted the language so well that hardly any subsequent modification has proved necessary. As Emile Benveniste wrote: 'un analyste moderne n'aurait presque rien à y changer' (quoted in Minassian, 1976: 31). The letters ֆ and Օ were added in the twelfth century, Օ representing a shift in the pronunciation of -av to /o/, while ֆ was introduced to denote /f/, a sound alien to Armenian, found in loan-words.

Punctuation marks:

full stop	:		
colon	·		
comma	,		
exclamation mark	՛	e.g. *աւաղ՛* /avagh/ 'alas!'
question mark	՞	e.g. *ի՞նչ* /inč/ 'what?'

THE ARMENIAN SCRIPT

THE ALPHABET

Capitals	Lower case	Transliteration	Cursive	
Ա	ա	a	Ա	ա
Բ	բ	b	Բ	բ
Գ	գ	g	Գ	գ
Դ	դ	d	Դ	դ
Ե	ե	e	Ե	ե
Զ	զ	z	Զ	զ
Է	է	ē	Է	է
Ը	ը	ə	Ը	ը
Թ	թ	t'	Թ	թ
Ժ	ժ	ž	Ժ	ժ
Ի	ի	i	Ի	ի
Լ	լ	l	Լ	լ
Խ	խ	x	Խ	խ
Ծ	ծ	c	Ծ	ծ
Կ	կ	k	Կ	կ
Հ	հ	h	Հ	հ
Ձ	ձ	j	Ձ	ձ
Ղ	ղ	ł	Ղ	ղ
Ճ	ճ	č	Ճ	ճ
Մ	մ	m	Մ	մ
Յ	յ	y	Յ	յ
Ն	ն	n	Ն	ն
Շ	շ	š	Շ	շ
Ո	ո	o	Ո	ո
Չ	չ	č'	Չ	չ
Պ	պ	p	Պ	պ
Ջ	ջ	ǰ	Ջ	ջ

7

Capitals	Lower case	Transliteration	Cursive	
Ռ	ռ	ṙ	*ո*	*ռ*
Ս	ս	s	*Ս*	*ս*
Վ	վ	v	*Վ*	*վ*
Տ	տ	t	*Տ*	*տ*
Ր	ր	r	*ր*	*ր*
Ց	ց	cʻ	*ց*	*ց*
Ւ	ւ	w	*ւ*	*ւ*
Փ	փ	pʻ	*փ*	*փ*
Ք	ք	kʻ	*ք*	*ք*

Source: Adapted from Minassian, M. (1976) *Manuel pratique d'Arménien ancien*, Paris, Librairie Klincksieck.

BATAK

Batak (also known as Toba) belongs to the Malayo-Polynesian branch of Austronesian. It is spoken by about 2½ to 3 million people in northern Sumatra. Much of the rich traditional literature of the Batak people has been recorded in a script based ultimately on an Indic model. The script is now losing ground to Roman.

THE BATAK SCRIPT

THE ALPHABET

‌	*a*	‌	*dja*
‌	*ha*	‌	*da*
‌	*ma*	‌	*nga*
‌	*na*	‌	*ba*
‌	*ra*	‌	*wa*
‌	*ta*	‌	*ja*
‌	*sa*	‌	*nja*
‌	*pa*	‌	*i*
‌	*la*	‌	*u*
‌	*ga*		

MEDIAL AND FINAL VOWELS

‌ -*i*   ‌ -*u*   ‌ -*o*   ‌ -*e*

‌ ‌ ‌ = *ripi*   ‌ = *pu*   ‌ = *bu*

‌ = *bo*   ‌ = *be*

pangolat ‌ makes consonant mute: ‌ ‌ ‌ = *rap*

hamisaran ‌ nasalization: ‌ = *bang;*   ‌ = *bing*

10

BENGALI

The derivative of Brāhmī in which Bengali (Bāṅlā) is written is also used for Assamese, Khasi and a few other local languages. The inherent vowel in any consonant, corresponding to Devanāgarī /a/ is /ɔ/: thus ক is /kɔ/. /ɔ/ alternates as inherent vowel, in consonants forming polysyllables, with /o/, but always in the sequence ɔ – o, never the reverse: thus, bɔṛo 'big', gɔrom 'hot'. This alternation forms part of the vocalic assimilation or 'vowel raising' which is a characteristic feature of Bengali phonology, and which can be broadly summarized as follows:

/ɔ, e, o/ → [o, i, u] if the following syllable contains /i/ or /u/

/i, u, e/ → [e, o, æ] if the following syllable contains /ɔ, a, e, o/

/a/ → [e] if the preceding syllable contains /i/

/a/ → [o] if the preceding syllable contains /u/

For example cali 'I go', is pronounced [coli], where inherent /ɔ/ is raised to [o] before /i/; similarly, from šona 'to hear', šuni 'I hear' (/o/ → [u] before /i/). The /ɔ/ → [o] and /e/ → [æ] shifts affect pronunciation only; the others are notated in the script.

Both short and long *i* and *u* still figure in the Bengali vocalic inventory, but the distinction in length is no longer phonologically significant.

In Bengali, as typically in the Magadhan daughter languages, the three sibilants of Sanskrit (dental, retroflex and palatal) have coalesced to yield /ʃ/, with a tendency towards /s/, especially in Bangladesh.

Conjunct consonants are formed, as in Devanāgarī, by means of juxtaposition and superimposition.

Other signs used in Bengali script:

Sanskrit *anusvāra*, Bengali ɔnušar: in Sanskrit, the sign ‸ , superscript above the letter which it follows, marks the unmodified nasal. In Bengali it is notated as ং and may be replaced in some words by the velar nasal ঙ. As in Devanāgarī, vowels may also be nasalized by the sign ঁ.

ঃ Sanskrit *visarga*, Bengali *biŝɔrgo*. In some Bengali words the sign indicates strong aspiration; in others it marks a lengthening of the preceding consonant. For rules of sandhi affecting visarga, see Devanāgarī.

◌্ *hasanta*. This corresponds to Devanāgarī virāma. It cancels the vowel sound inherent in a consonant:

Bengali ক্ = Devanāgarī क् /k/.

The accompanying table shows the consonantal inventory of Bengali, the independent vowels and the secondary vowel signs in combination with /k/.

THE BENGALI SCRIPT

CONSONANTS

ক *k*	খ *k*	গ *g*	ঘ *gh*	ঙ *ṅ*					
চ *c*	ছ *ch*	জ *j*	ঝ *jh*	ঞ *ñ*					
ট *ṭ*	ঠ *ṭh*	ড *ḍ*	ঢ *ḍh*	ণ *ṇ*					
ত *t*	থ *th*	দ *d*	ধ *dh*	ন *n*					
প *p*	ফ *ph*	ব *b*	ভ *bh*	ম *m*					
য় *y*	র *r*	ল *l*	ব *v*						
শ *ś*	ষ *ṣ*	স *s*	হ *h*	য *z*	ড় *ṛ*	ঢ় *ṛh*			

VOWELS

(a) independent:

অ *a*	আ *ā*	ই *i*	ঈ *ī*	উ *u*	ঊ *ū*	ঋ *ri*
এ *ē*	ঐ *ai*	ও *ō*	ঔ *au*	অং *aṅ*	অঃ *a'*	

(b) in combination with /k/:

কা *kā*	কি *ki*	কী *kī*	কু *ku*	কূ *kū*
কৃ *kri*	কে *kē*	কৈ *kai*	কো *kō*	কৌ *kau*

NUMERALS

১	২	৩	৪	৫	৬	৭	৮	৯	০
1	2	3	4	5	6	7	8	9	0

BERBER

Berber is a member of the Afro-Asiatic (Semito-Hamitic) family of languages. It seems to have been originally spoken in a strip of North African territory, stretching from the Atlantic coast to the borders of Egypt. Over the last thousand years, Berber-speaking populations have spread far beyond this original habitat, and today two or three hundred Berber dialects are spoken in about a dozen North African countries. The total number of Berber speakers is put at about 12 million. The principal dialects are Shluh, Tamazight and Riff in Morocco, Kabyle and Shawia in Algeria, Tamahaq (Tamashek or Tuareg) in several Saharan countries. All of these dialects are essentially spoken colloquials, with no written literature. Nevertheless, a script for the notation of Berber consonants had been devised more than 2,000 years ago, as is shown by two bilingual (Punic-Berber) inscriptions, found in the Roman city of Dugga in Tunisia. Many hundreds of Berber inscriptions have also been discovered in Libya. These are in Roman script, but are of great value as they are vowelled.

The two inscriptions found at Dugga are in a script identical, or at least very close, to the *tifinagh* script, which is still in use among the Tuareg people. The word tifinagh is the Tamahaq plural form of *tafineq*, which means 'letter', and is a berberization of the Latin word *punica*.

Tifinagh is a purely consonantal script, written from right to left. It has no way of indicating initial or medial short vowels, though the point called *tagherit* (see the accompanying table) may be used to indicate final /a, i/ or /uː/. Further, the letters : and ⟩ can be used as the counterparts of the Arabic /uː/ and /iː/. There is no way of indicating gemination, which is of phonemic importance in Berber.

THE BERBER SCRIPT

THE ALPHABET

Tar'erit		*a, i, u*	Iel	‖	*l*
Ieb	Ⅲ Ⓓ	*b*	Iem	⊐	*m*
Iet	+	*t*	Ien	Ⅰ	*n*
Ied	Π ∧ ⊔	*d*	Iek	∴	*k*
Iej	Ⅱ	*j*	Iak'	⋯	*q*
Iez	♯	*z*	Ier'	⋮	*ɣ*
Iez'	Ⅹ Ⅺ	*z'*	Iech	Ɔ	*ʃ*
Ier	□ ○	*r*	Iah	⋮	*h*
Ies	▣ ⊙	*s*	Iadh	Ⅎ	*ḍ, ṭ*
Ieg	⋰ ⋱	*g*	Iakh	∷	*χ*
Ieg'	⋈	*g'*	Iaou	:	*ū*
Ief	⊨ ⊫	*f*	Iéy	⩽	*ī*

COMBINED LETTERS

Iebt	+⊟	*bt*	Ielt	⊬	*lt*
Iezt	♯	*zt*	Iemt	+⊒	*mt*
Iert	⊞	*rt*	Ient	†	*nt*
Iest	+⊡	*st*	Iecht	+Ꝺ	*ʃt*
Iegt	⧺	*gt*	Ienk	⋰	*nk*
Ieg't	+⋈	*g't*			

Source: Hanoteau, A. (1890) *La Langue Tamachek*, Algiers.

BUGINESE

The Buginese-Maccasarese syllabary known in Buginese as *hurupu'*
sulapa' əppa' 'four-corner letters', is based on an Indian model, runs from
left to right, and retains the typically Indian system of marking non-inde-
pendent vowels as super-, subscript or collinear adjuncts to consonants.
From the accompanying chart it will be seen that the Devanāgarī velar,
labial, dental and palatal series are each represented by three consonants
(the aspirates are missing); and each row ends with a homorganic
conjunct: *ngka, mpa, nra, ɲca*. The inventory is completed by the four
semi-vowels *y, r, l, w*, the sibilant *s* and the spirant *h*. The letter ![symbol]
serves (a) to notate initial *'a/a*, and (b) to act as a carrier for other
vowel sounds in initial position. The vocalic diacritics are here shown in
combination with the consonant *la*:

| *la* | *li* | *lu* | *le* | *lo* | *lə* |
| la | li | lu | le | lo | lə |

Major defects in the script are its inability to notate independent vowels,
and the absence of markers denoting gemination, nasalization and
glottalization. Thus ![symbol] can be read as *sara* 'sorrow', *sara'* 'rule' and
sarang 'nest'. According to Sirk (1975) the conjunct graphs are not systematically used.

In Maccasarese, which does not have the vowel /ə/, the diacritic ◡ is
used to indicate that the syllable so marked is followed by a nasal consonant.

THE BUGINESE SCRIPT

THE SYLLABARY

ka	*pa*	*ta*	*ca*	*ya*	*sa*
ga	*ba*	*da*	*ja*	*ra*	*qa*
nga	*ma*	*na*	*ña*	*la*	*ha*
ngka	*mpa*	*nra*	*ñca*	*wa*	

BURMESE

Burmese (Myan-ma) belongs to the Burmic branch of the Tibeto-Burmese family. From south-west China, where its close congener, Yi, is still spoken, Burmese was carried southwards, to reach its present habitat by the ninth century AD. Here, it came into contact with the Mon language, and the Pali scriptures of Buddhism. The result was an amalgam: Tibeto-Burman stock with a Mon-Khmer substratum and writing system, plus a Pali-Buddhist ideological superstructure. The earliest written records in Burmese date from the eleventh century. By the twelfth century, Burmese had replaced Mon as the literary language of the Mon court.

The Burmese script is derived from the Mon version of Brāhmī. As in all Indic scripts, each base consonant has an inherent short vowel /a/. In addition to their primary forms, all vowels and certain consonants have secondary forms. The table shows the consonantal inventory of Burmese, and the initial vowel signs and the secondary vowel signs as applied to a consonant, denoted by C.

Eleven vowels are coded for tone, i.e. they require no tone marker. Seven of these are second tone, three are first tone, and one is third. Using /k/ as bearer consonant, we then have:

Second tone

      ကာ *kā*,   ကီ *kī*,   ကူ *kū*,   ကေ *kē*,   ကယ် *kɛ̄*,   ကော် *kɔ*,   ကို *kō*,

First tone

      က *ka*,   ကိ *ki*,   ကု *ku*,

Third tone

      ကဲ *kɛ̄*

First-tone vowels other than the three specified above are marked with subscript dot, e.g.

  ေက *ke,* ကဲ့ *kɛ,* ေကာ့ *kɔ,* ကို့ *ko.*

Third tone vowels are marked with **ː** (< Sanskrit visarga) e.g.

  ကား *kā,* ကီး *kī,* ကူး *kū,* ေကး *kē,*

THE BURMESE SCRIPT

CONSONANTS

က	ခ	ဂ	ဃ	င	စ	ဆ	ဇ	ဈ	ည	ဋ
ka	*kha*	*ga*	*ga*	*nga*	*sa*	*sa*	*za*	*za*	*nya*	*ta*
ဌ	ဍ	ဎ	ဏ	တ	ထ	ဒ	ဓ	န	ပ	
tha	*da*	*da*	*na*	*ta*	*tha*	*da*	*da*	*na*	*pa*	
ဖ	ဗ	ဘ	မ	ယ	ရ	လ	ဝ	သ	ဟ	ဠ
pha	*ba*	*ba*	*ma*	*ya*	*ya(ra)*	*la*	*wa*	*sa*	*ha*	*la*

VOWELS

(a) independent:

အ	အာ	အား	ဣ	ဤ	ဥ	ဦ
a	*ā*	*ā*	*i*	*ī*	*u*	*ū*

ဧ	ဧ	အဲ	ဩ	ဪ	ဩ	အံ
e	*ē*	*ɛ*	*ō*	*ō*	*ō*	*an*

(b) as used with bearer consonant, represented by C:

C -*a*   Cာ -*ā*   Cား -*ā*   Cိ -*i*   Cီ -*ī*   Cု (C౸) -*u*   Cူ (Cౖ) -*ū*

ေC -*e*   ေC -*ē*   Cဲ -*ɛ*   ေCာ် -*ō*   ေCာ -*ō*   Cိ -*ō*

CONJUNCT CONSONANTS

As a general rule, conjunct consonants retain their primary form and are written
as subscripts, but four – ya, ra, wa, ha – have specific forms, shown here as
applied to *ma*:

မ *ma*,   မျ *mya*,   မြ *mya*,   မွ *mwa*,   မှ *hma*,   မျွ *mywa*,   မျှ *hmya*,

မြှ *hmya*,   မွှ *hmwa*,   မြို *myo*.

NUMERALS

၁	၂	၃	၄	၅	၆	၇	၈	၉	၀
1	2	3	4	5	6	7	8	9	0

CAMBODIAN

Cambodian (Khmer) belongs to the Mon-Khmer sub-division of the Austro-Asiatic family. There are about 6 or 7 million speakers in Cambodia and Vietnam. The oldest inscriptions in Khmer date from the seventh century AD.

The Khmer script derives from a South Indian variant of Devanāgarī. The original Devanāgarī order is preserved (the retroflex and dental series have coalesced) as is the siting of the vowels; and, as in Devanāgarī, the consonants in their base state have a syllabic value, i.e. a back vowel inheres in each. Khmer use of this Indian material, however, introduces an essential innovation: the consonants are divided into two series or registers: the first series with base inherent vowel -*aa*; the second with base inherent vowel -*ɔɔ*. One and the same vowel sign is then realized differently depending on the series of the consonant which it vocalizes. Thus, the system doubles the vocalic inventory (Cambodian is very rich in vowels) by giving one specific value to a vowel sign following a series 1 consonant, and quite another value to the *same* vowel sign following a series 2 consonant. Formally, Series 1 consonants correspond to the original Devanāgarī voiceless stops with their aspirates (including the affricate series); Series 2 consonants correspond to the Devanāgarī voiced stops with their aspirates. For example, *kh* in series 1 represents Devanāgarī *kh*; *kh* in series 2 represents Devanāgarī *gh*. As illustration: *kh* in series 1 is ខ ; *kh* in series 2 is ឃ ; both can be followed by the vowel sign for long *ā*: ា : but ខាត់ is pronounced [khat] ('to polish'); ឃាត់ is pronounced [khoət] ('to prevent).

The consonantal phonemes of Cambodian are shown in the table. The phonemic values given are those of consonants preceding vowels. As first components in clusters, and as finals, the aspirated consonants are reduced to their non-aspirate values: /kh/ > /k/, etc.

The vowel symbols with their first and second series values are also set out in the table.

Some examples from the velar, palatal and dental series:

Series 1			Series 2		
ក	ក	/kɑɑ/ neck	គ	គ	/kɔɔ/ mute
ខ	ខាត់	/khat/ to polish	ឃ	ឃាត់	/khoǎt/ to prevent
ច	ចា	/caa/ to inscribe	ជ	ជា	/ciə/ be
ឆ	ឆោង	chaoŋ/ interval	ឈ	ឈោង	/chooŋ/ to reach out
ញ	ញុំ	/ñam/ to eat	ញ	ញុំ	/ñoǎm/ meat salad
ដ	ដុន	/don/ elephant command	ឌ	ឌុន	/dun/alike
ត	តា	/taa/ old man	ទ	ទា	/tiə/ duck

Source: Huffman, F.E. (1970) *Cambodian System of Writing, and Beginning Reader*. Yale University Press.

As can be seen from the consonant chart, certain Cambodian phonemes are not paired, e.g. series 2 *mɔɔ* has no series 1 correlative **maa*. Where it is necessary to produce such a correlative, a consonant can be 'converted' by diacritic: ″ converts a Series 2 into a Series 1 consonant, e.g.:

ម̎ = mɑɑ.

Similarly, ⌢ converts a Series 1 into a Series 2 consonant.

Conjunct consonants are frequent in Cambodian. The second component is written as a subscript, which is usually a reduced version of the base form. There are, however, several irregularities.

The value – i.e. whether it is to be read as series 1 or 2 – of a vowel following an initial or a medial cluster depends on the nature of the components forming the cluster. Very briefly, all stops and spirants take precedence over continuants, and therefore determine vocalic sequence. Thus, in /trəy/ 'fish' the series 1 stop /t/(taa) takes precedence over the continuant /r/ and requires the vowel /əy/.

Where two stops belonging to different series form a cluster, the subscript takes precedence. For instance, in /pteəh/ 'house' the series 2 subscript /t/(tɔɔ) prescribes the vowel; /ph/ > /p/ is a series 1 consonant.

THE CAMBODIAN SCRIPT

CONSONANTS

ក	kaa	k	ដ	daa	d	ប	baa	b
ខ	khaa	kh	ឋ (ឋ)	thaa	th	ភ	phaa	ph
គ	kɔɔ	k	ឌ	dɔɔ	d	ព	pɔɔ	p
ឃ	khɔɔ	kh	ឍ	thɔɔ	th	ភ	phɔɔ	ph
ង	ŋɔɔ	ŋ	ណ	naa	n	ម	mɔɔ	m
ច	caa	c	ត	taa	t	យ	yɔɔ	y
ឆ	chaa	ch	ថ	thaa	th	រ	rɔɔ	r
ជ	cɔɔ	c	ទ	tɔɔ	t	ល	lɔɔ	l
ឈ	chɔɔ	ch	ធ	thɔɔ	th	វ	wɔɔ	w
ញ	ñɔɔ	ñ	ន	nɔɔ	n	ស	saa	s
								ហ	haa	h
								ឡ	laa	l
								អ	qaa	q

Source: Huffman, F.E. (1970) *Cambodian System of Writing, and Beginning Reader.* Yale University Press.

VOWELS

Symbol	Name	Values 1st Series	Values 2st Series	Symbol	Name	Values 1st Series	Values 2st Series
—	sraq qɑɑ	aa	ɔɔ	ƒ -	sraq qei	ei	ee
-ɔ	sraq qaa	aa	iə	ƒ -	sraq qae	ae	εε
—	sraq qeq	e	i	ƒ -	sraq qay	ay	iy
—	sraq qəy	əy	ii	ƒ-ɔ	sraq qao	ao	oo
—	sraq qəq	ə	i	ƒ-ɔ	sraq qaw	aw	iw
—	sraq qəi	əi	ii	—	sraq qom	om	um
—	sraq qoq	o	u	—	sraq qɑm	am	um
—	sraq qou	ou	uu	-ɔ	sraq qam	am	oəm
—	sraq quə	uə	uə	-:	sraq qah	ah	eəh
ƒ -	sraq qaə	aə	əə				
ƒ-ɔ	sraq qiə	iə	iə				
ƒ-ɔ	sraq qiə	iə	iə				

Source: Huffman, F.E. (1970) *Cambodian System of Writing, and Beginning Reader*. Yale University Press.

CHEROKEE

Cherokee is a member of the Iroquoian group of the Macro-Siouan family. The language is spoken today – exclusively as a second language – by about 20,000 to 30,000 Cherokees in Oklahoma, with a residue in North Carolina. Ousted in tribal warfare from their original habitat in the Great Lakes area, the Cherokee moved south to Georgia and the Carolinas, where they proceeded to model their way of life and institutions on those of the European settlers. By the early 1800s they had achieved a remarkable degree of administrative, economic and cultural stability.

In 1819–20, Sequoyah, a Cherokee half-breed, invented a syllabary of eighty-six characters, some of which are borrowed from the Roman alphabet, though with different phonetic values. The spread of literacy in this script among the Cherokees was rapid, and in 1828 a Cherokee weekly newspaper, the *Cherokee Phoenix*, was launched, a unique event in the annals of the American Indian. Parts of the Bible, tracts and hymn-books soon appeared in the new script.

The script notates the vowels /a, e, i, o, u/ and /v/ = /$\tilde{\Lambda}$/, and seventy-nine combinations of consonant plus vowel. It does not notate vowel length, the intrusive /h/, or the glottal stop. It is partially inconsistent: e.g. in the velar series /ka/ and /ga/ are distinguished, the other five values are not.

THE CHEROKEE SCRIPT

THE SYLLABARY

D a		**R** e	**T** i	**Ꮙ** o	**Ꮳ** u	**i** v
Ꮟ ga	**Ꮞ** ka	**Ꮢ** ge	**Ꭹ** gi	**A** go	**J** gu	**E** gv
Ꮦ ha		**Ꮅ** he	**Ꮧ** hi	**Ꮺ** ho	**Ꮐ** hu	**Ꮒ** hv
W la		**Ꮷ** le	**Ꮅ** li	**Ꮹ** lo	**M** lu	**Ꮄ** lv
Ꮣ ma		**Ꮿ** me	**H** mi	**Ꮝ** mo	**Ꮍ** mu	
Ꮎ na	**Ꮏ** hna **Ꮐ** nah	**Ꮄ** ne	**Ꮒ** ni	**Z** no	**Ꮔ** nu	**Ꮕ** nv
Ꮖ qua		**Ꮌ** que	**Ꮗ** qui	**Ꮴ** quo	**Ꮎ** quu	**Ꮿ** quv
Ꮁ sa	**Ꮝ** s	**Ꮞ** se	**Ꮟ** si	**Ꮜ** so	**Ꮥ** su	**R** sv
Ꮣ da	**W** ta	**Ꮢ** de **Ꮦ** te	**Ꮧ** di **Ꮨ** ti	**V** do	**S** du	**Ꮩ** dv
Ꮸ dla	**Ꮃ** tla	**L** tle	**C** tli	**Ꮉ** tlo	**Ꮬ** tlu	**P** tlv
Ꮯ tsa		**Ꮴ** tse	**Ꮢ** tsi	**K** tso	**Ꮪ** tsu	**Ꮯ** tsv
Ꮹ wa		**Ꮺ** we	**Ꮻ** wi	**Ꮼ** wo	**Ꮽ** wu	**Ꮾ** wv
Ꮿ ya		**Ꮟ** ye	**Ꭹ** yi	**Ꮆ** yo	**Ꮍ** yu	**B** yv

Source: Holmes, R. B. and Smith, B. S. (1976) *Beginning Cherokee*, Norman, OK.

CHINESE

ARCHAIC

The earliest fragmentary examples of the Chinese writing system date from about 2000 BC. The first sizeable corpus of connected texts, however, is provided by the oracle inscriptions on animal bones and tortoise shells, which were used in divination rituals by the rulers of the Shang dynasty (c. 1400–1100 BC). From 1899 onwards, great numbers of these inscriptions have been excavated at the site of the ancient capital, Anyang, and elsewhere. Their content is largely stereotyped along the lines that one would expect to find in an economy based on agriculture: Is it going to rain? Will the harvest be plentiful? The question was apparently incised on one half of a shell, for example, which was then heated; the cracks which appeared in the other half were interpreted as the answer, and written in.

A typical oracle inscription falls into four sections: first, the day and place of the ritual are specified, the day being given in terms of the sixty-day cycle generated by the Ten (Heavenly Stems) and the Twelve (Earthly Branches); the name of the oracle may be added; this section always ends with the word *zhēn* 'asks'. The next section gives the text of the question, and the third section contains the answer, which is usually introduced by the stock phrase *wáng zhān yūe* 'the ruler read the answer'. Finally, the concluding section indicates the outcome of the prediction. While large numbers of inscriptions are identical as regards both content and form, small variations do occur; character sequence may change, certain words may be left out or replaced by others. Krjukov (1973) emphasizes the importance of this factor for close analysis of the Shang language. An example of a Shang oracle text is given on p. 28.

SCRIPT

The three basic elements – pictographs, ideographs and phonograms – of Chinese script are all present in the Shang script, which points to a lengthy period of anterior development.

Example of Shang oracle inscription (from Krjukov 1973):

㞢 ㋿ ㋿ X 㞢 ㋿ ㋿ ㋿ ㋿ X

du shou wo yu du bu wo ci shou yu

Glossary: *du* 'heaven'; *shou* 'give'; *wo* 'us'; *yu* 'help' *bu* 'not'; *ci*: an adverbial whose meaning is uncertain.

Translation: Will Heaven give us help? Heaven will not give us help.

Examples of pictographs are:

(= modern 馬 *mǎ*) 'horse';

(= modern 雨 *yǔ*) 'rain'.

Ideographs: e.g.

(= 下 *xià*) 'under, below';

(= 上 *shàng*) 'above, up'.

Phonograms: a phonogram is in origin a pictograph, chosen, for reasons which are not as yet clear, to notate a homophonic word. For example, the pictograph depicting the ear of wheat, came to be used to denote the word *lai* 'to come' (modern Chinese 來).

About 2,000 characters have been identified, a figure which represents a much larger corpus of 'words'. This is because the Shang characters (apart from the pronouns) might be described as semantically multivalued nuclei whose valencies depend on locus and function in the utterance as a whole. Thus, (= modern 子) can mean any of the following: 'son', 'filial', 'to be filial', 'to regard oneself as filial', 'befitting a son', etc. Up to a point, the modern Chinese graph shares the polyvalence characteristic of both Shang and Classical Chinese.

There is, however, an essential difference between the Shang character and its Classical/Modern Standard Chinese derivative. The Shang character for 'horse', for example (see above), is like a child's drawing of the animal: it is impressionistic, and the component strokes cannot be used to make other characters. In contrast, the character 馬 – standardized since the Shuo Wen dictionary of 100 AD (see Classical Chinese, below)

– is a conventional diagram: it is constructed according to a prescribed order of stroke, from a prescribed number of standardized elements – in this particular case, from three horizontal strokes $\equiv$, two vertical $| |$, one dextro-rotary angle $\exists$, and four dots ، ، ، ، . The graph 馬 is reducible to these elements, all of which are used consistently as components in thousands of other Chinese characters. The Shang graph is not so reducible. There was no consistency in character delineation, and variants abound.

In Modern Standard Chinese, again, the great majority of 'words' combine a semantic determinant – the radical – with a phonetic element. In Shang Chinese this combination is rare; according to Krjukov (1973), only about a dozen are to be found in the Anyang corpus. In these inscriptions we see the beginnings of the diachronic process which was to yield the typical Modern Standard Chinese 'word'.

Shang characters which share a phonetic element can, on that basis, be grouped as sharing some common feature of pronunciation. But exactly what that pronunciation was remains, at best, conjectural.

CLASSICAL (WENLI)

In a narrow sense, the term 'Classical Chinese' refers to the Chinese language and its literature from the sixth century BC to the third century AD; a period which includes the lives and works of Confucius, Mencius, Lao Tzu, Han Fei, Mo Tzu, and Chuang Tzu, to mention only the six philosopher-sages who were to have such a far-reaching effect on subsequent Chinese thought. In a broader sense, Classical Chinese begins with the *Shih Ching* ('Book of Odes'), which was compiled between the eleventh and sixth centuries BC, and which was in fact co-opted, during the central period, to form one of the 'Five Classics' (*wu jing*). The other four are:

I Jing ('Book of Changes');
Shu Jing ('Book of History');
Li Ji ('Book of Propriety');
Chun-Chiu ('Spring and Autumn Annals').

After the Burning of the Books by the Qin Emperor Shi Huang Di (213 BC), when most of this material was destroyed, the text of the Classics had to be arduously reconstructed. This took place in the early years of the Han Dynasty, whose espousal of Confucianism determined the lineaments of Chinese literature for many centuries to come. In the Confucian hegemony three factors were crucial: (1) the sacrosanctity of the classical texts; (2) the examination system based on these texts and their commentaries; (3) the supremacy of the literati who expounded the classics and set the examinations.

Outside the examination halls, a succession of poets – especially in the Tang and Sung Dynasties – some of them disreputable by Confucian standards, went on producing a lot of the world's most attractive poetry.

The main source for the character inventory used in the central Classical period is the *Shuo Wen* ('explain character') dictionary of the Later Han Dynasty (published c. AD 100). Here, the characters are arranged under 540 radicals (reduced to 214 in the late Ming Dynasty). The main categories of the *Shuo Wen* classification are:

1. Simple characters, a few hundred in number, sub-divided into

    (a) pictographs: e.g.

    木 *mù* 'tree';

    山 *shān* 'mountain';

    門 *mén* 'gateway, door';

    (b) demonstratives: e.g.

    二 *èr* 'two';

    上 *shàng* 'above',

    下 *xià* 'below'.

2. Compound characters, sub-divided into (a) ideograms, (b) phonograms:

    (a) ideograms are made from two or more simple characters; e.g.

    坐 *zuò* 'to sit' is formed from

    人 *rén* 'man', reduplicated, placed over

    土 *tǔ* 'earth.

    男 *nán* 'man', is made from

    田 *tián* 'field + 力 *lì* 'power'.

    (b) phonograms – the most numerous class – are made from two elements: the radical fixing the character as belonging to this or that semantic group, and the phonetic which suggests the pronunciation. Example:

聞 *wén* 'to hear':

composed of radical

耳 *ěr* 'ear' + 門 *mén*.

That is, the following information is given: the word has to do with hearing, and should rhyme with /mén/.

The nature of the script, and one standard method of looking up characters in a Chinese dictionary, are now illustrated by means of (a) eight full-form characters in bold printed form; (b) the same eight characters in standard written form (not in the so-called 'grass script' *cǎozi*, which is a highly personalized cursive); (c) stroke order and number; (d) the radical system; (e) search procedure in a Chinese dictionary.

(a)   Eight full-form printed characters:

中	海	茶	飯
zhōng	*hǎi*	*chá*	*fàn*
middle	sea	tea	food

錢	龍	聞	識
qián	*lóng*	*wén*	*shí*
money	dragon	hear	know

(b)   The same characters in standard written form:

中	海	茶	飯
zhōng	*hǎi*	*chá*	*fàn*

錢	龍	聞	識
qián	*lóng*	*wén*	*shí*

(c)   Stroke order is illustrated here by means of four of the above characters:

chá

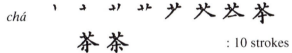

: 10 strokes

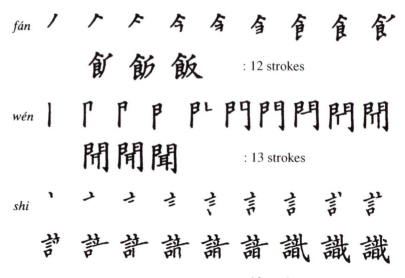

fán : 12 strokes

wén : 13 strokes

shi : 18 strokes

It will be seen that by writing a Chinese character in the correct *order*, we arrive at the correct *number* of component strokes. The number of components underlies both the radical system and the indexing of characters in a Chinese dictionary.

(d)   The radical system is set out on pp. 34–35 in traditional form, as a table of 214 radicals, beginning with one stroke and rising to seventeen. This is reproduced from Matthews' Chinese–English Dictionary. The radical table is followed by a specific example – the list of all characters having the seven-stroke radical 言 .

(e)   To sum up: looking up characters in a Chinese dictionary involves the following steps.

1.   Identify the radical; with experience this becomes automatic. The correct radical is usually obvious, but there are many cases where the radical is obscure, or where there is a choice.

2.   Count the strokes remaining in the character after the radical has been subtracted.

3.   Find the radical in the index of characters. All characters having this radical are listed in order of number of strokes; inspection in the correct section yields the desired character.

As example, we take the character 識 having the seven-stroke radical 言 . After subtraction of radical 149, the character has twelve strokes. By inspection in the twelve-stroke section of radical 149 we find 識 numbered 5825. Turning to 5825 in the body of the dictionary, we find the character with translation and many examples of usage.

THE 214 RADICALS

1 stroke

1	一
2	丨
3	丶
4	丿
5	乙
6	亅

2 strokes

7	二
8	亠
9	人 亻
10	儿
11	入
12	八
13	冂
14	冖
15	冫
16	几
17	凵

36	夕
37	大
38	女
39	子
40	宀
41	寸
42	小
43	尢兀尣
44	尸
45	屮
46	山
47	巛川巜
48	工
49	己
50	巾
51	干
52	幺
53	广
54	廴
55	廾
56	弋

74	月
75	木
76	欠
77	止
78	歹歺
79	殳
80	毋
81	比
82	毛
83	氏
84	气
85	水氵
86	火灬
87	爪
88	父
89	爻
90	爿
91	片
92	牙

110	矛
111	矢
112	石
113	示礻
114	内
115	禾
116	穴
117	立

6 strokes

118	竹⺮
119	米
120	糸糹
121	缶
122	网罒冈
123	羊
124	羽
125	老
126	而

7 strokes

147	見
148	角
149	言
150	谷
151	豆
152	豕
153	豸
154	貝
155	赤
156	走
157	足
158	身
159	車
160	辛
161	辰
162	辵辶
163	邑阝
164	酉
165	釆

181	頁
182	風
183	飛
184	食
185	首
186	香

10 strokes

187	馬
188	骨
189	高
190	髟
191	鬥
192	鬯
193	鬲
194	鬼

11 strokes

| 195 | 魚 |

14 strokes

| 209 | 鼻 |
| 210 | 齊 |

15 strokes

| 211 | 齒 |

16 strokes

| 212 | 龍 |
| 213 | 龜 |

17 strokes

| 214 | 龠 |

18 刀,刂	57 弓	93 牛,牜	127 禾	166 里	196 鳥
19 力	58 彐,彑	94 犬,犭	128 耳	*8 strokes*	197 鹵
20 勹	59 彡	*5 strokes*	129 聿	167 金	198 鹿
21 匕	60 彳	95 玄	130 肉,月	168 長,长	199 麥
22 匚	*4 strokes*	96 玉,王,王	131 臣	169 門	200 麻
23 匸	61 心,忄,⺗	97 瓜	132 自	170 阜,阝	*12 strokes*
24 十	62 戈	98 瓦	133 至	171 隶	201 黃
25 卜	63 戶	99 甘	134 臼	172 隹	202 黍
26 卩,㔾	64 手,扌	100 生	135 舌	173 雨,⻗	203 黑
27 厂	65 支	101 用	136 舛	174 青	204 黹
28 厶	66 攴,攵	102 田	137 舟	175 非	*13 strokes*
29 又	67 文	103 疋	138 艮	*9 strokes*	205 黽
3 strokes	68 斗	104 疒	139 色	176 面	206 鼎
30 口	69 斤	105 癶	140 艸,艹	177 革	207 鼓
31 囗	70 方	106 白	141 屯	178 韋	208 鼠
32 土	71 无,旡	107 皮	142 虫	179 韭	
33 士	72 日	108 皿	143 血	180 音	
34 夂	73 曰	109 目,⺫	144 行		
35 夊			145 衣,衤		
			146 襾		

RADICAL INDEX NOS. 147–150

6	討 6157	諒 3947	試 5798	諭 3423	謟 4468	譌 5795	**17** 識 181
	觧 5634	諄 1490	詣 3011	詞 2112	譣 5802	謁 7324	讒 161
7-18	訓 2914	論 4253	誅 1352	誌 2966	譗 7290	諫 847	護 3085
	訌 2385	謝 1591	詠 2308	詁 3461	膽 6185	謀 6322	讕 6066
	記 431	誶 5529	譽 111	詞 6971	瀟 1308	諼 4578	讟 3797
	訐 786	諏 6804	詿 2579	詁 131	譈 2273	諽 2875	
		調 6298	謟 2827	誚 1552	譙 4736	謹 5726	**18-22** 讟 2268
4	訛 4789	諉 7101	誅 4242	詐 5306	訣 4451	詼 2546	讚 6681
	訥 4609	註 2994	話 2215	評 5494	**11**	諡 5802	讖 7370
	訟 5558	詳 2108	誤 3329	誡 2864	謔 4823	諳 7538	讓 6096
	沈 5726	訛 6051	**7**	証 357	謞 279	誧 1362	讜 6522
	誡 2813	誃 5733	說 5939	謇 6956	誷 5674	諸 2839	**150** 谷 3483
	訐 2825	誅 3394	訴 2215	訖 6196	謷 62	謂 7079	
	訣 1700	詆 6078	語 7651	詠 7591	謾 4338	謚 7613	**14** 豊 7617
	訬 257	詔 370	誤 7204	誅 5147	譜 6734	証 2329	欬 2513
		詣 174	諧 3288	詈 3891		諾 4747	

觖 3587	
觭 5504	
觶 423	
觷 5136	
觳 2204	
觴 5668	
觶 970	
觶 3587	
觸 1416	
觿 2445	

COPTIC

Coptic – the latest form of Egyptian, which belongs to the Semito-Hamitic family – was widely spoken in Egypt from the third to the sixth centuries AD. It was never the language of administration, a role which the Greek introduced by the Ptolemies continued to discharge, even under the Roman Empire. From about 100 BC onwards, the old demotic script was discarded in favour of the Greek alphabetic script, and, with the spread of Christianity, Coptic began to acquire literary status. The translation of the Bible into Sahidic Coptic (mid-third century) was of enormous importance in this respect.

Thanks to the use of the Greek phonetic script, Coptic is the only form of Egyptian whose pronunciation is actually attested; hence the great importance of the language for Egyptian philology.

Seven additional letters were borrowed from Demotic (see **Egyptian**) to denote sounds alien to Greek: ꙍ / Ⱳ = /ʃ/, ꙅ = /f/, ꙧ = /ḫ/, ꙃ = ḫ, ⲭ = /dʒ/ȷ̌/ d′/, ꙉ = /k′/, ⳁ = /ti/.

z was probably pronounced as /z/, not /zd/ as in classical Greek, ꙃ = /ḥ/ is used for Greek ʻ (rough aspirate). The vowel marker ¯ indicates the reduced front vowel /ə/ pronounced before the bearer consonant: thus M = /əm/. Abbreviations are frequent, especially in the case of nomina sacra: e.g. IHⳙ = ICPⳗHⳙ 'Israel'; cꙍp = CꙍTHP 'saviour'.

Doubled vowels are read as vowel + hamza: BꙍꙍN = /boːʔon/ 'bad, evil'.

THE COPTIC SCRIPT

THE ALPHABET

Letter	Transcription	Letter	Transcription
Ⲁ ⲁ	a	Ⲣ ⲣ	r
Ⲃ ⲃ	b [b, v]	Ⲥ ⲥ	s
Ⲅ ⲅ	g	Ⲧ ⲧ	t
Ⲇ ⲇ	d	Ⲩ ⲩ	y [i, y]
Ⲉ ⲉ	e [ĕ]	Ⲫ ⲫ	ph [p + h]
Ⲍ ⲍ	z	Ⲭ ⲭ	kh [k + h]
Ⲏ ⲏ	ē	Ⲯ ⲯ	ps
Ⲑ ⲑ	th [t + h]	Ⲱ ⲱ	ō
Ⲓ ⲓ	i [i, j]	Ϣ ϣ	š
Ⲕ ⲕ	k	Ϥ ϥ	f
Ⲗ ⲗ	l	Ϧ ϧ	ḫ [ch]
Ⲙ ⲙ	m	Ϩ ϩ	h
Ⲛ ⲛ	n	Ϫ ϫ	dž
Ⲝ ⲝ	x [ks]	Ϭ ϭ	č
Ⲟ ⲟ	o [ŏ]	Ϯ ϯ	ti
Ⲡ ⲡ	p		

CREE

This is the major language of the Algonquian family in North America. It is spoken by about 60,000 Indians over a vast territory, extending from Hudson's Bay in the east, across Ontario and Manitoba to Saskatchewan and Alberta, and from the grain belt northwards to Mackenzie and Kewatin.

The Cree syllabary was developed by the Rev. James Evans in the 1830s, and by 1840 it was being used to print religious texts in Cree. As further modified and improved by the Rev. John Horden (author of *A Cree Grammar*), the syllabary has been subsequently used for the considerable body of Biblical translation and original devotional literature published in Cree from the late nineteenth century onwards.

THE CREE SCRIPT

THE SYLLABARY

	e'	i	o	a	Finals	
					Moose (M)	Western (W)
Independent Vowel	▽	△	▷	◁		
p	V	∧	>	<	<	ǀ
t	U	∩	)	(	ᴄ	/
c	⌐	⌐	⅃	∪	∪	_
k	ᑫ	ᑭ	ᑯ	ᑲ	ᑊ	∖
m	˥	Γ	⅃	L	L	ᴄ
n	ᓀ	ᓯ	ᓓ	ᓇ	ᓇ	⊃
l	⊃	⊂	⊐	⊏	⊏	{
s	ᔦ	ᔨ	ᔪ	ᔭ	ᔮ	⌒
š	ᔓ	ʃ	∿	ᔑ	ᔑ	
y	◁ᐠ	ᐁ	◁	ᐢ	°	•
r	⌣	⌢	ᑎ	ᕓ	ᕐ	}

CYRILLIC

The earliest Old Slavonic texts, dating from the tenth century AD, are written in two alphabets, Glagolitic and Cyrillic. The former seems to have been the earlier of the two. Both alphabets are attributed to the 'Apostles to the Slavs', the brothers St Cyril and St Methodius, Greeks who were active as linguists and missionaries in Moravia in the middle of the ninth century.

As a basis, the apostles used the Greek uncial alphabet, necessarily amplified with letters denoting specifically Slavonic phonemes. Two letters were borrowed from Hebrew to denote /tʃ/ and /ʃ/: **צ** (*tsade*) > **ч**, **ש** (*shin*) > **ш**. Letters were also invented for the nasal vowels of Old Church Slavonic, and for short /ŭ/ and /ĭ/. The Cyrillic version of the Old Church Slavonic alphabet is set out in the accompanying table.

With the conversion of Vladimir I of Kiev to Christianity in 989, and the consequent adherence of the Kievan principality to the Greek Orthodox communion, a wide new field for the dissemination of the scriptures was opened up. The Cyrillic script now spread into the East Slavonic speech area, for which, as a South Slavonic medium, it had not been originally designed. In point of fact, however, early writing through the Kievan and Mongol periods (eleventh to fourteenth centuries) continued to be largely in Old Church Slavonic; and the prevalence of a south Slavonic language written in a South Slavonic script was fortuitously reinforced by an influx of South Slavonic clerics after the fall of Constantinople in 1453.

If the Old Church Slavonic language was exclusively used for ecclesiastical texts, Old Russian steadily gained ground as the medium for lay material. In this new context, the Old Church Slavonic letters for the nasal vowels became superfluous and fell into disuse, while certain other letters acquired new functions: notably those for short /ŭ/ and /ĭ/ (**ъ** and **ь**), which came to denote hard or soft syllable closure: cf. Old Church Slavonic Пѫть /pătĭ/ 'way, path', Russian Путь /putʲ/.

The first years of the seventeenth century saw the onset of the *smutnoje vremja* the 'time of troubles' in the Muscovite state, leading to the *raskol*, the 'great schism' in the Russian church – twin developments which weakened the ecclesiastical hegemony, and opened the door towards secularization. Old Russian was used for several polemical works, some of which are of considerable literary value. Worthy of special mention in this context is the *Uloženie*, or 'Code of Tsar Alexis' (1649), a code of law written in the Muscovite vernacular of the mid-seventeenth century. This work enjoyed official status and wide dissemination for almost 200 years, and had an important influence on the emergent Russian literary language. In this seminal role, the *Uloženie* has been compared with Luther's translation of the Bible. Simplification and secularization of the Cyrillic script came with Peter the Great's educational reforms in the early years of the eighteenth century. The Petrine 'civil alphabet', the *graždanskaja azbuka*, now entered on its new secular career, in the early stages of which book production in Russia was to rise from seven volumes a year in 1725 to about 5,000 a year by 1800. The script itself remained unchanged until the 1917 Revolution, when five letters – і, ъ, ѣ, ѳ, ѵ – were discarded as redundant, though ъ was subsequently reinstated. The contemporary inventory is set out in the accompanying Cyrillic table.

The Russian vocalic system is systematically divided into hard and soft series, specifically notated in the Cyrillic script as follows:

hard: ы /ɨ/, э /ɛ/, а /a/, о /o/ у /u/

soft: и /i/, е /je/, я /ja/ ё /jo/, ю /ju/

One extremely important feature of the Russian vowel system is not reflected in the script. This is the extensive reductionism which affects all unstressed vowels except /u/. In particular, unstressed /o/ tends to become [a]: this phenomenon is known as *akanje*. Where two or more unstressed vowels (not /u/) precede the tonic stress, the reductionist process is graduated through more than one stage of the secondary vowel inventory. This is particularly evident in the case of /o/: cf. *xorošo* /xərʌʃó/ 'well, good'; *golova* /gəlʌvá/ 'head'.

The five East and South Slav nations which are in communion with the Greek Orthodox Church use the Cyrillic script with certain modifications:

Ukrainian: ё, ъ; ы, Э are dropped, Є /je/, і /i/, ї /ji/ are added. Thus 'Kiev' is written as Київ; 'Europe' as Європа/jevropa/

Belorussian: И is dropped, і and ў /w/ are added.

Serbian: the 1818 dictionary of Vuk Stefan Karadžić introduced an adapted Cyrillic, including the following new letters:

Ћ ћ /ć/, Џ џ /dʒ/, Ђ ђ /đ/

Љ љ /lj/ Њ њ /nj/

43

Bulgarian: ё, ы, Э are dropped. The hard sign ъ is used to denote the typically Bulgarian phoneme /ʌ/ > /ə/.

Macedonian: has the following additions:

ѓ /dj/, Ј /j/, Љ /lj/ Њ /nj/, ќ /tj/, Џ /dʒ/, Ѕ /dz/.

The Cyrillic script as applied to the non-Slavonic languages of the Russian Federation of States: before the 1917 Revolution the Arabic script was used for the written languages of the Islamic peoples in Central Asia and the Caucasus. The 1930s saw an extensive experimental programme of romanization, which was soon abandoned; and Cyrillic alphabets were then devised for all the written languages of the Soviet Union. Most of these are currently in use.

The considerable difficulties involved in adapting the Cyrillic script to the needs of markedly different phonological systems – e.g. those of the Caucasian languages – were approached (a) by introducing new characters, and (b) by modifying and/or combining existing characters. Thus, Roman capital I was introduced to notate the ubiquitous (in Caucasian languages) hamza-onset and ejective articulation.

The Turkic languages of the Russian Federation of States all use Cyrillic plus supplementary letters. Most of the Turkic languages have about half a dozen such letters. Kazakh has nine:

ә г қ ң ө ұ ү һ і

Other languages of the Russian Federation of States: to the Cyrillic base, Nenets, for example, adds ' for the nasal glottal stop, and " for the oral glottal stop. Nivkh uses ' to mark aspiration, and distinguishes the velar pair /k/, /g/ from the uvular pair /q/, /G/, which are notated as *k̦*, *r̦*. The voiced velar fricative /ɣ/ is denoted by ҕ; the uvular counterpart /ʁ/ by ҕ.

THE OLD CHURCH SLAVONIC SCRIPT

THE ALPHABET

Name	Symbol		Transliteration	Name	Symbol		Transliteration
As	Ⰰ	Ⰰ	a	Chʲer	Х	χ	kh
Buki	Б	Ɓ	b	O	Ꙩ	ꙩ	o
Wʲedi	Ⰲ	в	v	Tßi	Ц	ц	c
Glagolʲ	Г	г	g	Tscherwʲ	Ч	ч	č
Dobro	Д	д	d	Scha	Ш	ш	š
Eßtʲ	Ⰵ	є	e	Schta	Щ	щ	št
Żiwʲete	Ж	ж	ž	Jer	Ъ	ъ	ŭ
Zʲelo	Ѕ	ѕ	dʃ	Jery	{ Ꙑ / Ы	ꙑ / ы }	y
Semlja	З	з	ʃ				
Iže	И	и	i	Jerek	Ь	ь	ĭ
I	I	і	i	Jetʲ	Ѣ	ѣ	ě
Kako	К	к	k	Ju	Ю	ю	ju
Ljudi	Л	л	l	Ja	Ꙗ	ꙗ	ja
Myslite	М	м	m	Je	Ѥ	ѥ	je
Nasch	Н	н	n	Ęß	Ѧ	ѧ	ę
On	О	о	o	Ąß	Ѫ	ѫ	ǫ
Pokoj	П	п	p	Jęß	Ѩ	ѩ	ję
Rtßi	Р	ρ	r	Jąß	Ѭ	ѭ	jǫ
Sslovo	С	с	ß	Kßi	Ѯ	ѯ	kß
Twerdo	Т	т	t	Pßi	Ѱ	ѱ	ps
Uk	{ Ꙋ / Оу	ꙋ / оу }	u	Thita	Ѳ	ѳ	f/θ
Fert	Ф	ф	f	Ižitßa	V	ѵ	ẏ [i]

45

THE CYRILLIC SCRIPT

THE ALPHABET

Printed		Handwritten		Transliteration
А	а	*A*	*a*	a
Б	б	*Б*	*б*	b
В	в	*В*	*в*	v
Г	г	*Г*	*г*	g
Д	д	*Д*	*д*	d
Е	е	*Е*	*е*	e
Ё	ё	*Ё*	*ё*	ë
Ж	ж	*Ж*	*ж*	ž
З	з	*З*	*з*	z
И	и	*И*	*и*	i
Й	й	*Й*	*й*	j
К	к	*К*	*к*	k
Л	л	*Л*	*л*	l
М	м	*М*	*м*	m
Н	н	*Н*	*н*	n
О	о	*О*	*о*	o
П	п	*П*	*п*	p
Р	р	*Р*	*р*	r
С	с	*С*	*с*	s
Т	т	*Т*	*т*	t
У	у	*У*	*у*	u
Ф	ф	*Ф*	*ф*	f
Х	х	*Х*	*х*	x
Ц	ц	*Ц*	*ц*	c
Ч	ч	*Ч*	*ч*	č
Ш	ш	*Ш*	*ш*	š
Щ	щ	*Щ*	*щ*	šč
	ъ		*ъ*	"
	ы		*ы*	y
	ь		*ь*	'
Э	э	*Э*	*э*	e
Ю	ю	*Ю*	*ю*	ju
Я	я	*Я*	*я*	ja

Source: Comrie, B. (1987) 'Russian', in B. Comrie (ed.) *The World's Major Languages*, London, Routledge.

DEVANĀGARĪ

The Devanāgarī script is the most important derivative of the Brāhmī script, itself a left-to-right adaptation of a right-to-left Semitic script, which seems to have been introduced into north-west India from Mesopotamia early in the first millennium BC. The Devanāgarī letters used for Sanskrit date from the eighth century AD. The name may be translated as 'sacred city writing' or 'city writing of the gods' (Macdonell 1924); *deva* 'divine, god', *nāgara* 'urban'. The thirty-four consonants and thirteen vowels of the script are set out in the accompanying chart, plus the vowels in combination with /k/:

का	कॉ	कि	कॊ	कु	कू	कृ	कॄ	कॢ
kā	kāṁ	ki	kī	ku	kū	kṛ	kṝ	kḷ

Conjunct consonants are formed by juxtaposition and or superimposition (often involving some deformation). Some representative examples follow:

क्त	क्र	क्ष	ज्ञ	त्र	त्व	द्य	द्र	द्व	प्त
kta	kra	kṣa	jña	tra	tva	dya	dra	dva	pta

ब्द	र्क	र्कं	श्च	श्र	श्व	स्त	स्य	स्र	स्व
bda	rka	rkaṁ	śca	śra	śva	sta	sya	sra	sva

ह्म	ह्य	ह्र	ह्ल	ह्व	त्स्न्य
hma	hya	hra	hla	hva	rtsnya

virāma: this is a slanting stroke drawn to the bottom right of a consonant to indicate cancellation of the inherent /a/: thus,

तत् = *tat*

anusvāra: a dot over a consonant or vowel indicating nasalization:

अं = *aṁ*,   कं = *kaṁ*

pre- and post-consonantal r: r preceding a consonant is written as ˤ above the consonant; thus,

र्म = *rma*,   र्क = *rka*

r following a consonant is written as a short stroke slanting to the left from the lower part of the consonant:

क्र = *kra*,   प्र = *pra*

Devanāgarī is used to write several modern Indian languages. By far the most important is Hindi.

47

THE DEVANĀGARĪ SCRIPT

VOWELS (SVARĀH)

अ	आ	इ	ई	उ	ऊ
a	ā	i	ī	u	ū

ऋ	ॠ	ऌ	ए	ऐ	ओ	औ
ṛ	ṝ	ḷ	e	ai	o	au

CONSONANTS (VYAÑJANĀNI)

Stops (sparśāḥ)					Semi-vowels (antaḥsthāḥ)	Spirants (ūṣmāṇaḥ)	Others
क	ख	ग	घ	ङ		ह	:
k	kh	g	gh	ṅ		h	ḥ
च	छ	ज	झ	ञ	य	श	
c	ch	j	jh	ñ	y	ś	
ट	ठ	ड	ढ	ण	र	ष	ळ
ṭ	ṭh	ḍ	ḍh	ṇ	r	ṣ	ḷ
त	थ	द	ध	न	ल	स	
t	th .	d	dh	n	l	s	
प	फ	ब	भ	म	व		
p	ph	b	bh	m	v		

Source: Cardona, G. (1987) 'Sanskrit' in B. Comrie (ed.) *The World's Major Languages*, London, Routledge.

NUMERALS

१	२	३	४	५	६	७	८	९	०
1	2	3	4	5	6	7	8	9	0

EGYPTIAN

One of the oldest attested languages in the world, Egyptian belonged to the Afro-Asiatic family, and showed several features shared in common with Semitic. The following stages in the development of Egyptian are distinguished:

1. Old Egyptian of the third millennium BC. Known from the Pyramid Texts, the most archaic form of Egyptian, and from funerary inscriptions of the fifth and sixth Dynasties.
2. Classical or Middle Egyptian, covering the period 2240–1780 BC (Dynasties 9 to 12).
3. Late Classical: 1780–1350 BC (Dynasties 13 to 18). The *Book of the Dead* was compiled in this period.
4. Late Egyptian: fourteenth to eighth centuries BC (Dynasties 18 to 24).
5. Demotic: eighth century BC to fifth century AD.
6. Coptic.

The 'sacred writing' deciphered by Champollion in the 1820s is known as hieroglyphic. Several thousand hieroglyphs are known, many of them being very rare or *hapax legomena*. The hieroglyphic script is sub-divided into:

(a) Ideograms: these represent objects in purely graphic fashion with no phonetic element; e.g.

 ⊙ /rʿ/, 'day, sun';

 ⊐ /pr/, 'house'.

(b) Phonograms: these are particularized signs indicating pronunciation; e.g.

 ⟾ /r/, 'mouth'

comes to function in the course of the centuries as the conventional sign for /r/, and a series of such single-valued signs ultimately produces an alphabet (see below). At no stage of Egyptian before Coptic are vowels notated. To facilitate pronunciation, modern practice is to vocalize the Egyptian consonants with /e/. Thus, *pr* is read as /per/; *sn* 'brother', as /sen/, *nfr* 'beautiful' as /nefer/.

(c)   Syllabic signs representing two or three consonants, often accompanied by phonograms: Thus,

�container /nb/, 'basket';

★   /sb'/, 'star'/

(d)   Determinatives: these are class or function markers posted at words to suggest their semantic field. Thus, verbs of motion are often accompanied by the determinative

Λ

and words denoting liquids by the determinative

〰〰〰

(cf. Chinese radicals, which have a similar function, though they are, of course, shorthand for characters with phonetic values). An Egyptian determinative when acting as such, has no phonetic role; it may, however, be particularized to define the object represented: it is then accompanied by a vertical stroke. Thus in

 /wbn/, 'rise, shine',

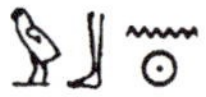

the sign

⊙

is a determinative with no phonetic value; in

⊙ /r'/

it is particularized to denote 'the sun'. Thus, a sign may function in three different ways – as ideogram, as phonogram, and as determinative.

The Egyptian script is read either vertically downwards, or horizontally left to right or right to left. Ideograms representing gods, humans, or animals act as pointers to the direction in which the script is to be read: if they face to the right of the viewer, the script is read from right to left, and vice versa. Symmetry of a purely formal nature plays an important part in the arrangement of signs. There is no punctuation.

A cursive form of hieroglyphic, known as hieratic, is attested from about 3000 BC. An abbreviated cursive, known as demotic, appears from about 800 BC onwards. While there is a one-to-one correspondence between a hieroglyph and its hieratic version, there is no such correspondence in demotic script, which is full of ligatures.

THE EGYPTIAN SCRIPT

THE ALPHABET

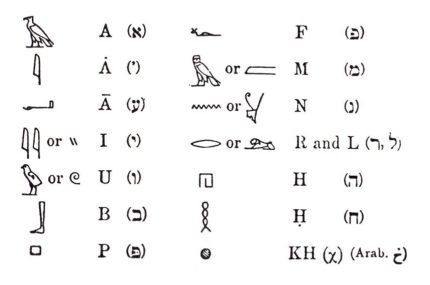

	A (א)		F (פ)	
	Ȧ (’)	or	M (מ)	
	Ā (ע)	or	N (נ)	
or	I (י)	or	R and L (ר, ל)	
or	U (ו)		H (ה)	
	B (ב)		Ḥ (ח)	
	P (פ)		KH (χ) (Arab. خ)	

	S (ס)		Ḳ (ק)
	S (שׁ)		T (ת)
	SH (Ś) (שׁ)		Ṭ (ט)
	K (כ)		TH (θ) (ת)
	Q (ק)		TCH (T’) (צ)

Source: Budge, W. (1978) *The Egyptian Language*, London, Routledge.

EPIGRAPHIC SOUTH ARABIAN

From the middle of the second millennium BC onwards, a group of highly civilized city-states developed in the south-west corner of the Arabian peninsula (corresponding roughly to modern Yemen), the most notable being Saba', Ma'īn, Qatabān and Ḥaḍramawt. The inhabitants of these states spoke Sabaean, Minaean, Qatabanian and Ḥaḍrami, all four being dialects of the language known as Epigraphic South Arabian. The economic success and stability of these states was based on intensive irrigation, agriculture and an extensive network of trade-routes. The account given in I Kings, chapter 10, of the visit of the Queen of Sheba (Saba') to King Solomon provides a fascinating glimpse of life at the top in tenth-century Arabia. Gradually through the first millennium BC the city-states declined in power and prestige, to be replaced (second century BC) by the Ḥimyaritic state, which preserved, along with a Sabaean-type dialect, much of Sabaean culture. In addition to the four dialects listed above, the group includes the nucleus of what was to become Ge'ez, the classical language of Ethiopia. The epigraphic record points to the colonization of Ethiopia from south-west Arabia early in the first millennium BC.

The consonantal alphabet, which was used to write inscriptions in the South Arabian languages, is set out in the accompanying chart. This shows the monumental character typical of the older inscriptions (eighth century BC onwards), with some examples, in parentheses, of forms assumed in the later cursive. The reconstruction of South Arabian phonology and morphology is hampered by the absence of signs for the short vowels and for gemination. The exact function of the consonants *w* and *y* is not clear. In forms like -*hw* (3rd person singular masculine suffix) and *ywm* (singular noun 'day'), *w* appears to denote long /u/.

Basically the script runs from right to left. Boustrophedon texts are also found, especially in the older period. In these, non-symmetric characters such as ⧊ (*m*) and ⋈ (*d*) are reversed: ⧊, ⋈ so as to face right on the return line (cf. the similar practice as regards anthropomorphic characters, gods and men, in Egyptian hieroglyphic).

Several thousand South Arabian inscriptions of varying length (some very long) are known. They comprise oracular and votive texts, spells, incantations, military records, administrative edicts, legal documents, graffiti, burial inscriptions, etc. Two definitive collections are:

1. *Corpus inscriptionum semiticarum ad academia inscriptionum et literarum conduit atque digestum, Parisiis. Pars quarta inscriptiones himyariticas et sabaeas continens*, vols I–III. Paris, 1889–1932.
2. *'Répértoire d'épigraphie semitique' publié par la Commission du Corpus Inscriptionum Semiticarum*, vols V–VII, ed. G. Ryckmans (Inscriptions sud-arabes, Nos 2624–5106). Paris, 1929–50.

The first has photographs giving the epigraphic text plus transliteration; the second has transliteration only. See also Conti Rossini (1931), Beeston (1937).

THE EPIGRAPHIC SOUTH ARABIAN SCRIPT

ʾ	Ⴖ	(ⴤ)	m	ⴸ	( )))
b	Ⴖ	(ⴔ)	n	Ⴑ	(ⴆ)
g	ⴕ		s(?)	Ⴖ	
d	ⴸ		c	o	
ḏ	Ⴑ		ġ	ⴕⴕ	
h	Ⴘ		f	◊	
w	ⴲ		ṣ	ⴖ	(ⴽ)
z	ⴸ		ḍ	Ⴒ	
ḥ	ⴘ	(ⴘ)	q	ⴔ	(ⴅ)
ḫ	ⴖ		ẓ	)	(ⴒ)
ṭ	ⴒ	(ⴒ)	š(?)	ⴹ	
ẓ	ⴖ		ś(?)	ⴴ	
y	ⴕ	(9)	t	ⴴ	(ⴵ)
k	ⴖ	(ⴶ)	ṯ	ⴘ	
l	ⴕ				

Source: Bauer, G.M. (1966) *Jazyk južnoaravijskoj pis'mennosti*, Moscow.

ETHIOPIC

The Ethiopic syllabary is derived from the South Arabian consonantal script, which was used in south-west Arabia from about 1500 BC to the second century BC (see **Epigraphic South Arabian**). Through the first millennium BC, Ethiopia was gradually colonized by Sabaean merchants and settlers, who brought with them the nucleus of what was to become Ge'ez, the classical language of Ethiopia.

By the fourth century AD, the South Arabian script, as used in the Aksumite state in Ethiopia (by then Christianized), had undergone two modifications of fundamental importance: the direction of writing was reversed, possibly under the influence of Greek, to run from left to right, in place of the typically Semitic right to left; second, the consonantal graphs were individually modulated, so as to notate their vocalization. Thus arose the Ethiopic syllabary of seven vocalic orders, which is set out in the accompanying table. The first of the seven orders consists of the base form of the consonant with the inherent vowel /a/.

Five Sabaean letters were discarded as superfluous in Ethiopic, while six new letters were introduced: four of these denote the labialized velar phonemes $q°$, $h°$, $k°$, $g°$. As will be seen from the table, these do not have forms for the second and seventh orders, as labialization *per se* involves the rounded vowels /u/ and /o/.

Serious shortcomings in the Ethiopic script are: (1) the absence of some means of denoting the gemination which is so important, usually phonemic, both in Ethiopic itself and in the daughter languages. In the seventeenth century an attempt was made to remedy this defect by introducing the Arabic *tashdid* but this did not catch on. (2) Similarly, Ethiopic has nothing corresponding to the Arabic *sukun*, used to indicate that the bearer consonant is vowelless. Where conjunct non-vocalized consonants occur, e.g. in words like *medr* 'earth', *sayf* 'sword', the convention is to write them in the sixth order, i.e. with short *e*: thus, *medr* is written as *medere*, and correct reading as *medr* depends on the reader's awareness that the only possible pattern (Arabic *wazn*, *awzān*) here is $C_1eC_2C_3$ medr.

The Ethiopic syllabary is used to write the daughter languages Amharic, Tigrinya and Tigre, and has been used for other languages such as Somali and Oromo (Galla). In the case of Amharic, the syllabary was, early in the seventeenth century, extended by seven letters denoting specifically Amharic phonemes.

THE ETHIOPIC SCRIPT

THE SYLLABARY

	a		ū		ī		ā		ē		e		ō
ሀ	ha	ሁ	hū	ሂ	hī	ሃ	hā	ሄ	hē	ህ	he	ሆ	hō
ለ	la	ሉ	lū	ሊ	lī	ላ	lā	ሌ	lē	ል	le	ሎ	lō
ሐ	ḥa	ሑ	ḥū	ሒ	ḥī	ሓ	ḥā	ሔ	ḥē	ሕ	ḥe	ሖ	ḥō
መ	ma	ሙ	mū	ሚ	mī	ማ	mā	ሜ	mē	ም	me	ሞ	mō
ሠ	ša	ሡ	šū	ሢ	šī	ሣ	šā	ሤ	šē	ሥ	še	ሦ	šō
ረ	ra	ሩ	rū	ሪ	rī	ራ	rā	ሬ	rē	ር	re	ሮ	rō
ሰ	sa	ሱ	sū	ሲ	sī	ሳ	sā	ሴ	sē	ስ	se	ሶ	sō
ቀ	qa	ቁ	qū	ቂ	qī	ቃ	qā	ቄ	qē	ቅ	qe	ቆ	qō
በ	ba	ቡ	bū	ቢ	bī	ባ	bā	ቤ	bē	ብ	be	ቦ	bō
ተ	ta	ቱ	tū	ቲ	tī	ታ	tā	ቴ	tē	ት	te	ቶ	tō
ኀ	ḫa	ኁ	ḫū	ኂ	ḫī	ኃ	ḫā	ኄ	ḫē	ኅ	ḫe	ኆ	ḫō
ነ	na	ኑ	nū	ኒ	nī	ና	nā'	ኔ	nē	ን	ne	ኖ	nō
አ	'a	ኡ	'ū	ኢ	'ī	ኣ	ā	ኤ	'ē	እ	'e	ኦ	'ō
ከ	ka	ኩ	kū	ኪ	kī	ካ	kā	ኬ	kē	ክ	ke	ኮ	kō
ወ	wa	ዉ	wū	ዊ	wī	ዋ	wā	ዌ	wē	ው	we	ዎ	wō
ዐ	'a	ዑ	'ū	ዒ	'ī	ዓ	'ā	ዔ	'ē	ዕ	'e	ዖ	'ō
ዘ	za	ዙ	zū	ዚ	zī	ዛ	zā	ዜ	zē	ዝ	ze	ዞ	zō
የ	ja	ዩ	jū	ዪ	jī	ያ	jā	ዬ	jē	ይ	je	ዮ	jō
ደ	da	ዱ	dū	ዲ	dī	ዳ	dā	ዴ	dē	ድ	de	ዶ	dō
ገ	ga	ጉ	gū	ጊ	gī	ጋ	gā	ጌ	gē	ግ	ge	ጎ	gō
ጠ	ṭa	ጡ	ṭū	ጢ	ṭī	ጣ	ṭā	ጤ	ṭē	ጥ	ṭe	ጦ	ṭō
ጰ	pa	ጱ	pū	ጲ	pī	ጳ	pā	ጴ	pē	ጵ	pe	ጶ	pō
ጸ	ṣa	ጹ	ṣū	ጺ	ṣī	ጻ	ṣā	ጼ	ṣē	ጽ	ṣe	ጾ	ṣō
ፀ	ḍa	ፁ	ḍū	ፂ	ḍī	ፃ	ḍā	ፄ	ḍē	ፅ	ḍe	ፆ	ḍō
ፈ	fa	ፉ	fū	ፊ	fī	ፋ	fā	ፌ	fē	ፍ	fe	ፎ	fō
ፐ	pa	ፑ	pū	ፒ	pī	ፓ	pā	ፔ	pē	ፕ	pe	ፖ	pō

THE LABIALIZED VELAR SERIES

ኰ	*kua*	ኵ	*kuī*	ኵ	*kue*	ኳ	*kuā*	ኴ	*kuē*
ጐ	*gua*	ጕ	*guī*	ጕ	*gue*	ጓ	*guā*	ጔ	*guē*
ቈ	*qua*	ቍ	*quī*	ቍ	*que*	ቋ	*quā*	ቌ	*quē*
ኈ	*ḫua*	ኍ	*ḫuī*	ኍ	*ḫue*	ኋ	*ḫuā*	ኌ	*ḫuē*

GEORGIAN

Georgia was converted to Christianity in the middle of the fourth century; and a need to make the Gospels accessible to the Georgians in their own language must have fostered the creation of a Georgian alphabet, which followed early in the fifth century. According to tradition, St Mesrop Mashtotz, the creator of the Armenian script, was also, at least in part, responsible for the Georgian alphabet. Like the Armenian, the Georgian alphabet is clearly based on a Greek model, for example in the order of the letters. But the Georgian phonological inventory is very different from the Greek; and this first classification and notation of Caucasian phonemes – a classification which remains valid today – must rank as a linguistic achievement of the first order.

This early Georgian alphabet is known as *xucuri*. In the eleventh century, it was replaced by the *mxedruli* 'civil' script. Seven of the original forty mxedruli letters are now obsolete. The thirty-three letters now in use are shown in the table. Punctuation follows the West European model.

THE GEORGIAN SCRIPT

THE ALPHABET

ა	a	რ	r
ბ	b	ს	s
გ	g	ტ	ṭ
დ	d	უ	u
ე	e	ფ	ph
ვ	v	ქ	kh
ზ	z	ღ	γ
თ	th	ყ	q
ი	i	შ	ʃ
კ	ḳ	ჩ	čh
ლ	l	ც	ts
მ	m	ძ	dz
ნ	n	წ	ṭs
ო	o	ჭ	tʃ
პ	p	ხ	χ
ჟ	ž	ჯ	dž
		ჰ	h

GOTHIC

Gothic belongs to the Germanic branch of Indo-European. In the fourth century AD, the Visigoths were settled along the lower course of the Danube and in neighbouring areas, and it was here that Bishop Wulfila worked as missionary and translator, first north of the Danube, and after 348 south of the river in Roman territory. Wulfila seems to have translated most of the Bible into Gothic, and our knowledge of the language rests on the extensive fragments which have survived. The manuscripts date from about the sixth century, and were found in northern Italy, brought there presumably by the Ostrogoths. The script used is, basically, a Greek uncial plus graphs from Roman and Runic (*u* and *o*).

THE GOTHIC SCRIPT

THE ALPHABET

ᚨ	Ᏼ	Γ	ᴅ	Ɇ
a	b	g	d	e

ᴜ	Ꮓ	𝒽	ѱ	ᴵ ï
q	z	h	θ	i

ᴋ	ᴧ	ᴍ	ᴎ	ɢ
k	l	m	n	j

ᴨ	Π	ᴿ	Ꙅ	ᴛ
u	p	r	s	t

Ƴ	Ϝ	Χ	Θ	Ω
w	f	ch	hw	o

GREEK

Ancient Greek was first written, from c. 1400 to the twelfth century BC, in the Mycenaean script known as Linear B. This is the script which was deciphered by Ventris and Chadwick in 1952. An earlier script, associated with the Minoan culture of Crete, has not been deciphered; the language it notates is probably non-Indo-European.

The Mycenaean script was a syllabary, similar in structure to those used in Japanese. Independent vowels could be notated, especially if initial, but not independent consonants. Thus Ancient Greek words appear in Linear B exactly as Anglo-American loan-words do in Japanese katakana: e.g. *elektryōn* appears as *a.re.ku.tu.ru.wo*. In the same way, katakana writes *sukottorando* for 'Scotland', and *happibaasudee* for 'happy birthday'.

The Mycenaean script did not survive the Dorian invasions of Greece. When written Greek re-appears, in the eighth century, it is in an alphabetic script based on a North Semitic model. To begin with, the Semitic direction of writing – right to left – was copied, with frequent use of boustrophedon. After about 500, the left-to-right mode became standardized. Symbols for non-Semitic phonemes were invented. But the truly momentous step was taken when letters for the five vowels a, e, i, o, u were introduced. This far-reaching innovation ensured that the Greek alphabetic script would become – particularly after it came into Roman hands – the most successful and the most practically useful of the world's scripts. Not phonologically the most precise: here, the Graeco-Roman script must take second place to Devanāgarī. But no other script has been called upon to serve so many widely differing sound systems (though the closely related Cyrillic is a close second). The Greek script which was adopted in Athens in 403, and thereafter generalized, was, in terms of Greek dialectology, an Ionic (Eastern) model. The pitch accents – acute, grave and circumflex – were introduced in the third century. The table shows the Greek letters, upper and lower case, with their ancient and modern pronunciation.

THE GREEK SCRIPT

THE ALPHABET

Capital letter	Small Letter	Ancient phonetics	Usual transliteration	Modern pronunciation	Usual transliteration
A	α	[a]	a	[a]	a
B	β	[b]	b	[v]	v
Γ	γ	[g]	g	{ [j] (/—i,e) [γ] (elsewhere)	y g(h)
Δ	δ	[d]	d	[ð]	d(h)
E	ε	[ε]	e	[ε]	e
Z	ζ	[zd]	z	[z]	z
H	η	[ε:]	e:, ē	[i]	i
Θ	θ	[tʰ]	th	[θ]	th
I	ι	[i]	i	[i]	i
K	κ	[k]	k	[k]	k
Λ	λ	[l]	l	[l]	l
M	μ	[m]	m	[m]	m
N	ν	[n]	n	[n]	n
Ξ	ξ	[ks]	x	[ks]	ks, x (as in *box*)
O	o	[o]	o	[o]	o
Π	π	[p]	p	[p]	p
P	ϱ	[r]	r	[ɾ]	r
Σ	σ (ς)	[s]	s	[s]	s
T	τ	[t]	t	[t]	t
Y	υ	[y]	y, u	[i]	i
Φ	φ	[pʰ]	ph	[f]	f
X	χ	[kʰ]	ch, kh	[χ]	h, x (IPA value)
Ψ	ψ	[ps]	ps	[ps]	ps
Ω	ω	[ɔ:]	o:, ō	[o]	o

Diphthongs and clusters	Ancient phonetics	Usual transliteration	Modern pronunciation	Usual transliteration
αι	[aι̯]	ai	[ε]	e
αυ	[au̯]	au	[av] (/__ + voice)	av
			[af] (/__ − voice)	af
ει	[eː]	ei	[i]	i
ευ	[εu̯]	eu	[ev] (/__ + voice)	ev
			[ef] (/__ − voice)	ef
οι	[oι̯]	oi	[i]	i
ου	[oː]	ou	[u]	u
υι	[yι̯]	yi, ui	[i]	i
γ before γ χ ξ	[ŋ]	n (g, kh, ks)	[ŋ]	n (g, h, ks)
γκ	[ŋk]	nk	[(ŋ)g] (medially)	(n)g
			[g] (initially)	g
μπ/μβ	[mp/mb]	mp/mb	[(m)b] (medially)	(m)b
			[b] (initially)	b
ντ/νδ	[nt/nd]	nt/nd	[(n)d] (medially)	(n)d
			[d] (initially)	d
τζ	-----	-----	[dz]	dz

Source: Joseph, B.D. (1987) 'Greek', in B. Comrie (ed.) *The World's Major Languages*, London, Routledge.

GUJARATI

Gujarati (Gujarātī) is a New Indo-Aryan language, which took shape from a western form of Middle Indian around the eleventh/twelfth century AD. Literature in Gujarati begins to appear in the fifteenth century, and about the same time in the closely cognate Rajasthani. But whereas Rajasthani stuck to Devanāgarī, Gujarati, for its part, developed a graceful cursive script which dispenses with the superscript bar, characteristic of Devanāgarī. The only other New Indo-Aryan script which is closely similar to the Gujarati is the Kaithi cursive script, sometimes used for writing Hindi in northern India.

The table shows the Gujarati consonantal inventory, and the vowels: the latter (a) in their independent forms, and (b) in combination with the consonant *b*. Like other Brāhmī derivatives, the Gujarati script is syllabic, with short *a* inherent in each consonant.

Conjunct consonants are formed by juxtaposition, partial amalgamation or subscript.

As in Devanāgarī, the inherent vowel is cancelled by virāma ◥. The final *ḥ* in Sanskrit words is denoted by : visarga, and ◡ anusvāra marks nasalization which is homogeneous with the following consonant.

THE GUJARATI SCRIPT

CONSONANTS

ક	ખ	ગ	ધ	ઽં
ka	kha	ga	gha	nga

ચ	છ	જ	ઝ	ઞ
ca	cha	ja	jha	nya

ટ	ઠ	ડ	ઢ	ણ
ṭa	ṭha	ḍa	ḍha	ṇa

ત	થ	દ	ધ	ન
ta	tha	da	dha	na

પ	ફ	બ	ભ	મ
pa	pha	ba	bha	ma

ય	ર	લ	વ	
ya	ra	la	wa, va	

શ	ષ	સ	હ	ળ
śa	ṣa	sa	ha	la

VOWELS

(a) independent:

અ	આ	ઇ	ઈ	ઉ	ઊ	ઋ
a	ā	i	ī	u	ū	ri

એ	ઐ	ઓ	ઔ
ē	ai	ō	au

(b) in combination with the consonant *ba*:

બા	બિ	બી	બુ	બૂ	બૃ
bā	bi	bī	bu	bū	bri

બે	બૈ	બો	બૌ
bē	bai	bō	bau

NUMERALS

૧	૨	૩	૪	૫	૬	૭	૮	૯	૦
1	2	3	4	5	6	7	8	9	0

GURMUKHI

The emergence of the Gurmukhi (Panjabi) script is closely associated with the rise of the Sikh religion in the sixteenth century. Earlier, the defective North Indian script known as Landa had been used for Old Panjabi texts. The earliest Sikh teachers set about improving and rationalizing Landa on the Devanāgarī model. Thus enhanced, the *guru-mukhī* (literally, 'from the mouth of the teacher') script was used to write the text of the Adi Granth, the 'Original Book' of the Sikh religion, containing hymns by Guru Nānak (1469–1539), Arjan (1563–1606) and several other teachers. Gurmukhi is the script now used for the Panjabi language in India. In Pakistan, Panjabi is written in the Arabo-Persian character. The accompanying table shows the consonantal inventory of Indian Panjabi.

As in all scripts ultimately deriving from Brāhmī, each consonantal graph has an inherent vowel; in the case of Panjabi, this is short *ă* or /ə/. The lay-out of the letters is, in general, close to that of Devanāgarī, but there are two important special features:

(a) Three letters are used to provide bases for free-standing vowels. These are:

ੳ ūṛā   ਅ āiṛā   ੲ īṛī

As illustration, the vowel signs are now shown in combination with the consonant /kă/:

ਕ   ਕਾ   ਕਿ   ਕੀ   ਕੁ   ਕੂ   ਕੇ   ਕੈ   ਕੋ   ਕੌ

ka   *kā*   *ki*   *kī*   *ku*   *kū*   *kē*   *kai*   *kō*   *kau*

(b) Panjabi has three tones. Neutral tone is unmarked. A vowel following an initial voiced aspirate is in the low tone. [ha] is then mute, and the aspirate becomes its unvoiced counterpart: e.g. the script form [ghora:] is realized as /kòra:/ 'horse'. Cf. [ghaṛ] > /kàṛ/'house'. In final position, the same voiced aspirates and [ha] mark the preceding vowel as high e.g. [ca:h] is realized as /cá:/ 'tea'; the [ha] is again mute. Cf. kujh] ⲭ /kúj/ 'something'.

There are very few conjunct consonants in Panjabi. In general, for C_1C_2, C_1 is in base form, C_2 is attached in schematic outline. Specific subscript forms are used for *ra*, *wa*, *ha*.

THE GURMUKHI SCRIPT

CONSONANTS

ਸ	ਹ			
sa	*ha*			

ਕ	ਖ	ਗ	ਘ	ਙ
ka	*kha*	*ga*	*gha*	*nga*

ਚ	ਛ	ਜ	ਝ	ਞ
ca	*cha*	*ja*	*jha*	*nya*

ਟ	ਠ	ਡ	ਢ	ਣ
ṭa	*ṭha*	*ḍa*	*ḍha*	*ṇa*

ਤ	ਥ	ਦ	ਧ	ਨ
ta	*tha*	*da*	*dha*	*na*

ਪ	ਫ	ਬ	ਭ	ਮ
pa	*pha*	*ba*	*bha*	*ma*

ਯ	ਰ	ਲ	ਵ	ੜ
ya	*ra*	*la*	*va*	*ṛa*

HEBREW

The north-western branch of Semitic, as it appears at the turn of the second and first millennia BC, falls into two main groups, Aramaic and Canaanite. By far the most important member of the latter group is Hebrew, known from a vast literature, central to which is the Old Testament (earliest material c. 1200 BC, latest c. 200 BC). For most of the first millennium BC, Hebrew epigraphic material is written in an Old Hebrew character, which was adapted from the Phoenician alphabet around 1000 BC. Circa 200 BC, however, a cognate form of Phoenician-based script was borrowed from Aramaic, and all subsequent Hebrew writing is in this 'square' character. The Samaritans alone retained the Old Hebrew form (see **Samaritan**).

The first table shows the Hebrew consonants with the Phoenician equivalents. It will be seen that five characters – kaf, mem, nun, pe and tsade – have two forms: the second form (in parentheses) is word-final only. Originally vowels were not marked. In the pre-Exilic period, three consonants, yod, waw and he, came to be used as *matres lectionis* for the notation of long final vowels: yod representing /iː, eː/, waw /oː, uː/ and he /aː/. Later, this usage was extended to medial long vowels.

In the seventh century AD, the Masoretes – Jewish scholars working to preserve the Hebrew text of the Old Testament with maximum fidelity – introduced the system of vocalization known as the Masoretic. Since the consonantal structure of the text was held to be sacred, and could not be modified in any way, vowel points were written above or below the consonants (but see Daghesh, below). The classical vocalization thus preserved represents, therefore, the pronunciation of Hebrew in the seventh century AD, and there are grounds for believing that the original pronunciation of the language was somewhat different. In addition to the *matres lectionis* for long vowels, the Masoretic system marks short /i, e, a, o, u/, plus simple shwa and three shwa augments /ĕ, ă, ŏ/. See the table of Hebrew vowels.

70

Daghesh. The single point written within a consonant, known as daghesh, has two functions:

(a) it distinguishes a stop from its correlative spirant, which has no point (daghesh lene):

$$t\ ת\quad t\ תּ\quad p\ (ף)פ\quad p\ פּ\quad k\ (ך)כ\quad k\ (ךּ)כּ$$

$$d\ ד\quad d\ דּ\quad g\ ג\quad g\ גּ\quad b\ ב\quad b\ בּ$$

(b) it marks gemination (daghesh forte), e.g.:

$$\ldots qq\ קּ\quad \ldots mm\ מּ\quad \ldots ww\ וּ\quad \ldots bb\ בּ$$

The letter shin is pointed at the upper left to notate /s/, at the upper right to notate /ʃ/:

$$שׂ\ s\quad שׁ\ \int$$

The sign ְ has a dual function: (a) it denotes the shwa vowel /ŏ/; and (b) it marks a medial consonant with null vocalization. In certain cases, there may be some doubt as to the correct reading. A useful rule is that ְ in a syllable following a long vowel always denotes /ŏ/.

Throughout the post-Biblical period and the Middle Ages, the 'vowel letters', waw for *o/u*, yod for *i*, were increasingly used in prose, though verse was more conservative. In the nineteenth and mid-twentieth century, a conservative orthography known as *xaser*, which used classical spelling without pointing, received scholarly sanction. At the same time, however, the press and the public in general stuck to *male*, a simplified orthography making extensive use of the vowel letters.

In 1970 the Hebrew Language Academy published rules for a standardized orthography without pointing.

YIDDISH

The many innovations in the Hebrew script as applied to Yiddish are primarily due to the difficulties inherent in the use of a Semitic notation for an Indo-European phonology. In particular, the *scripta plena* used for Yiddish is largely an imitation of German orthography, dating from the time of the Haskalah movement in the eighteenth century, which took up many of the ideas of the German *Aufklärung*. The Yiddish script is shown in the accompanying table. Letters marked with ** are used as word-finals only. In some forms of written Yiddish, letters marked with * occur only in quotations from Classical Hebrew literature.

It will be seen from the Yiddish table that alef is generalized as /a/, alef plus qāmeṣ is generalized as /ɔ/, and 'ayin as /e/. Cf.

דער מאַן   *der man* 'the man'

די פֿרוי   *di froj* 'the woman'

דאָס קינד   *dos kind* 'the child'

Various combinations are used to denote German diphthongs, e.g. double yod plus paṭaḥ = /aj/. Beth is generalized as /b/, i.e. the voiced stop only, the correlative fricative /v/ being represented by double waw. Initial alef before yod, waw or a diphthong is silent.

THE HEBREW SCRIPT

CONSONANTS

Phoenician (= Old Hebrew)	Jewish Square (modern print)	Cursive (modern)	Name	Transcription
☖	א	k	alef	?
٩	ב	⁊	bet	$B; b, b \sim v$
∧	ג	∂	g'imel	$G; g, g$
△	ד	⁊	d'alet	$D; d, d$
੧	ה	⋒	he	$H; h$
Y	ו	/	vav	$W; w \sim v, u, o$
I	ז	⅄	z'ayin	$Z; z$
႓	ח	n	xet	$H; h \sim x$
⊕	ט	6	tet	$T; t \sim t$
੧	י	'	yod	$Y; y, i,e$
⅄	כ (ך)	⊃(P)	kaf	$K; k, k \sim x$
ι	ל	✓	l'amed	$L; l$
⅍	מ (ם)	N(P)	mem	$M; m$
৭	נ (ן)	J(l)	nun	$N; n$
‡	ס	0	s'amex	$S; s$
O	ע	8	'ayin	'
٦	פ (ף)	∂(⅂)	pe	$P; p, p \sim f$
٢	צ (ץ)	3(⅄)	tsade	$S; s \sim c(=ts)$
φ	ק	ʔ	qof	$Q; q \sim k$
⅄	ר	⁊	resh	$R; r$
W	ש	e	shin	$Š; š$
X	ת	ɳ	tav	$T; t, t \sim t$

VOWELS

(a) The Masoretic vowels (without *matres lections*). C stands for consonant.

qāmeṣ:	subscript lateral plus vertical:	C̤
ṣēre:	two subscript dots:	C̤
ḥīreq:	one subscript dot:	C̣
ḥolem:	one superscript dot:	Ċ
paṭah:	one subscript lateral:	C̱
səghol:	two plus one subscript dots:	C̤
qibbuṣ:	three subscript dots in right-slanting line:	C

See examples below.

(b) The vowels (combining with various consonants).

Long		Short	Ultrashort
ṭå טָ		ṭa טַ	'ǎ עֲ
lēʸ לֵי	lē לֵ	lε לֶ	ʔɛ̌ אֱ
mōʷ מוֹ	rō רֹ	ṣå צָ	ḥǎ חֲ
tīʸ תִי		si סִ	zə, z ז
nūʷ נוּ		nu נֻ	

Source: Hetzron, R. (1987) 'Hebrew', in B. Comrie (ed.) *The World's Major Languages*, London, Routledge.

74

THE YIDDISH SCRIPT

THE ALPHABET

א	a	ח *	x(ch)	ס	s
אָ	o	ט	t	ע	e
ב (בֿ)	b	טש	č	פּ	p
ג	g	יִ, י	i, j	ף **, פֿ	f
ד	d	יי	ej	ץ **, צ	c
ה	h	יַי	aj	ק	k
ו, וּ	u	ך **, כ	x(ch)	ר	r
וי	oj	ל	l	ש	š
וו	v	ם **, מ	m	שׂ *	s
ז	z	ן **, נ	n	תּ *	t
זש	ž			ת *	s

Source: *Jazyki narodov CCCR*, Vol. 1, Moscow, 1966–80.

JAPANESE

The Joomon and Yayoi Neolithic cultures flourished in Japan from about 6000 BC to the fourth century AD. Nothing is known about their languages, and they seem to have left no written record in the form of inscriptions. Old Japanese, as it first appears in documents of the seventh/eighth centuries, is characterized by a sparse phonological inventory, a polysyllabic lexical structure and an agglutinative morphology, features which qualify the language equally well for inclusion in either the Altaic or the Malayo-Polynesian areal types. Japanese philologists have been much concerned with identifying 'Yamato' words – i.e. pristine Japanese words – as the core of the language. As attested, however, even the oldest stratum of the language does not seem to be entirely free of Chinese loan-words.

The Chinese morphemic script reached Japan via Korea in the third/fourth century AD. For Japanese, a polysyllabic and highly inflected language, a logographic script such as the Chinese character, perfectly adapted to a monosyllabic isolating language devoid of inflections, could be utilized in either or both of two ways:

(a) Chinese characters could be used to designate their Japanese semantic equivalents. This is known as the *kun* method. For example, the Chinese character 山 /shan/ in Chinese, meaning 'mountain', could be read as *yama*, the Japanese semantic equivalent. Early kun texts often stick awkwardly close to the syntactically alien Chinese text: e.g. negation markers are found preceding verbs, a word order which is characteristic of Chinese, not of Japanese. The artificial language thus produced is known as *kanbun*. A modified form of kanbun known as *hentai kanbun*, while retaining the principle of semantic transfer, tended to replace Chinese syntax with Japanese.

(b) *man'yoogana:* the *kun* method worked up to a point with bare stems. For the representation of Japanese inflections and particles, the man'yoogana method was developed: this involved selecting Chinese characters, regardless of meaning, as phonetic approximations: for example, the Japanese genitive/relative particle の /no/ is often represented in kanbun by 之 (zhi), its Chinese semantic equivalent. In man`yoogana writing, /no/ is represented by a Tang Chinese character, selected on grounds of phonetic similarity. In the same way, a Japanese polysyllabic word could be represented by a concatenation of Chinese phonetic approximations. It was an unwieldy method of writing, and there was no consistency in the selection of Chinese characters: at least a dozen Chinese graphs are used to denote the Japanese particle *ka*.

(c)   The ninth century saw the introduction of the *okototen* system, whereby Chinese characters used as kun (see above) were supplied with peripheral dots indicating which Japanese inflections or particles were to be added to complete the sense. Thus, if we use a square □ to represent a Chinese character, a dot at the upper right-hand corner □˙ indicates that the Japanese object marker (*w*)*o* is to be added. Similarly, a dot at the lower right-hand corner signals addition of the nominalizer *wa,* while a dot at the bottom left-hand corner marks the Japanese participial form in -*te*, and so on. At least eight key markers in Japanese morphology and syntax could be specified in this way.

(d)   At the same time, the two Japanese syllabaries, katakana and hiragana, were beginning to take shape. Katakana originated in abbreviated forms of Chinese characters, used as a kind of shorthand for mnemonic purposes. The elegant and aesthetically pleasing hiragana syllabary derives from the cursive writing of Chinese characters. Through the late Heian and the Kamakura periods – i.e. well into the Japanese Middle Ages – literature continued to be produced in a variety of scripts: in kanbun (mainly by Buddhist priests), in pure Chinese and in katakana (by male scholars and courtiers), and in hiragana (by ladies of the imperial court, among whom the Lady Murasaki Shikibu and the Lady Sei Shoonagon cannot fail to be mentioned). By the close of the Heian period, however, the so-called *wabun* style, based on hiragana plus a limited use of Chinese characters, had established itself as the most satisfactory medium for the notation of Japanese. Printing was imported from Korea in 1593. Early books are set in wabun style, the kanji being accompanied by furigana (phonetic glosses in hiragana), where required.

Modern Japanese (*hyoojungo* 'standard language') is written in a combination of Chinese characters and the two syllabaries. Hiragana is used for verbal inflection, nominal particles and many native Japanese words. Katakana is used for foreign words, particularly the Anglo-American words which proliferate in modern Japanese. It is also the script for telegraphese. Chinese characters function as root words, both verbal and nominal. For example, in the complex verb form *asobanakereba nari-masen* 'has/have to play', the root *aso-* 'play' is notated as the Chinese character 遊 (Chinese *you* 'to play') while the remaining ten syllables (final *-n* is syllabic), conveying the negative conditional and the negative present indicative, are in hiragana. Most Chinese characters used in Japanese have more than one pronunciation; as at the outset, over a thousand years ago, the basic distinction is still between the Sino-Japanese reading (the *on-yomi*) and the native Japanese reading (the *kun-yomi*). For example, the on-yomi reading of the character meaning 'to play', given above, is *yū*. Reference to this character in the dictionary (Nr. 4726 in Nelson's *Japanese–English Dictionary*) will show that out of about eighty compounds listed, only 25 per cent or so give 遊 its kun-yomi pronunciation (*aso-*); everywhere else, the on-yomi reading *yū-* is used.

In 1946, an official list of 1,850 Chinese characters was adopted as the desirable inventory for everyday purposes. In 1981, this list was extended to almost 2,000. Chinese characters not included in this list are accompanied, when used in print, by their hiragana readings.

The hiragana and katakana syllabaries are set out in the tables. For the structure of Chinese characters, see **Chinese**.

Extensive adoption of American-English loan-words has led in recent years to the introduction of several innovative katakana forms, denoting, for example, /ʃe/, /tʃɛ/, /wi/.

THE JAPANESE SCRIPT

THE SYLLABARIES

HIRAGANA

あ a	か ka	が ga	さ sa	ざ za	た ta	だ da	な na	は ha	ば ba	ぱ pa	ま ma	ら ra	わ wa	ん n
い i	き ki	ぎ gi	し shi	じ ji	ち chi	ぢ ji	に ni	ひ hi	び bi	ぴ pi	み mi	り ri		
う u	く ku	ぐ gu	す su	ず zu	つ tsu	づ zu	ぬ nu	ふ fu	ぶ bu	ぷ pu	む mu	る ru		
え e	け ke	げ ge	せ se	ぜ ze	て te	で de	ね ne	へ he	べ be	ぺ pe	め me	れ re		
お o	こ ko	ご go	そ so	ぞ zo	と to	ど do	の no	ほ ho	ぼ bo	ぽ po	も mo	ろ ro		を o
や ya	きゃ kya	ぎゃ gya	しゃ sha	じゃ ja	ちゃ cha	ぢゃ ja	にゃ nya	ひゃ hya	びゃ bya	ぴゃ pya	みゃ mya	りゃ rya		
ゆ yu	きゅ kyu	ぎゅ gyu	しゅ shu	じゅ ju	ちゅ chu	ぢゅ ju	にゅ nyu	ひゅ hyu	びゅ byu	ぴゅ pyu	みゅ myu	りゅ ryu		
よ yo	きょ kyo	ぎょ gyo	しょ sho	じょ jo	ちょ cho	ぢょ jo	にょ nyo	ひょ hyo ·	びょ byo	ぴょ pyo	みょ myo	りょ ryo		

KATAKANA

ア	カ	ガ	サ	ザ	タ	ダ	ナ	ハ	バ	パ	マ	ラ	ワ	ファ	ン
a	ka	ga	sa	za	ta	da	na	ha	ba	pa	ma	ra	wa	fa	n
イ	キ	ギ	シ	ジ	チ	ヂ	ニ	ヒ	ビ	ピ	ミ	リ		フィ	
i	ki	gi	shi	ji	chi	ji	ni	hi	bi	pi	mi	ri		fi	
ウ	ク	グ	ス	ズ	ツ	ヅ	ヌ	フ	ブ	プ	ム	ル			
u	ku	gu	su	zu	tsu	zu	nu	fu	bu	pu	mu	ru			
エ	ケ	ゲ	セ	ゼ	テ	デ	ネ	ヘ	ベ	ペ	メ	レ		フェ	
e	ke	ge	se	ze	te	de	ne	he	be	pe	me	re		fe	
オ	コ	ゴ	ソ	ゾ	ト	ド	ノ	ホ	ボ	ポ	モ	ロ		フォ	ヲ
o	ko	go	so	zo	to	do	no	ho	bo	po	mo	ro		fo	o

ヤ	キャ	ギャ	シャ	ジャ	チャ	ヂャ	ニャ	ヒャ	ビャ	ピャ	ミャ	リャ
ya	kya	gya	sha	ja	cha	ja	nya	hya	bya	pya	mya	rya
ユ	キュ	ギュ	シュ	ジュ	チュ	ヂュ	ニュ	ヒュ	ビュ	ピュ	ミュ	リュ
yu	kyu	gyu	shu	ju	chu	ju	nyu	hyu	byu	pyu	myu	ryu
ヨ	キョ	ギョ	ショ	ジョ	チョ	ヂョ	ニョ	ヒョ	ビョ	ピョ	ミョ	リョ
yo	kyo	gyo	sho	jo	cho	jo	nyo	hyo	byo	pyo	myo	ryo

Long vowels are notated in Hiragana by adding あ, い, う, え, or お, e.g.

おかあさん *okā-san;*

and in Katakana by adding ─, e.g.

テーブル *tēburu.*

Syllabic final consonants other than /n/ are notated

by つ in Hiragana

and by ツ in Katakana, e.g.

いった *itta*, and マッチ *matchi.*

JAVANESE

The Old Javanese literary language is attested from the tenth century AD. It is known as Kawi (< Sanskrit *kavi* 'sage, seer, poet'), and it was written in a script which is clearly based on Brāhmī. The same script was used for Old Balinese and Sundanese. Typically Indic features in the script are: (a) its syllabic character: as in Devanāgarī the vowel /a/ inheres in all base-form consonants; (b) the consonantal inventory is ordered in positional (velar, palatal, dental, labial) rows, each of five terms (see **Devanāgarī**); in Kawi, however, the retroflex series is represented by *ṭa* and *ḍa* only.

Also characteristically Indic is the presence of signs for /ṛ/ and /ḷ/ and for the three sibilants /s/, /ʃ/ and /ṣ/; also for anusvāra, visarga and virāma (see **Devanāgarī**).

An innovation in Kawi is the presence of signs for short and long /ə/, absent in the Brāhmī model.

With thirty-one consonantal and twenty vocalic symbols, the Kawi script was well equipped to notate a literary language, about 90 per cent of whose vocabulary consisted of Sanskrit loan-words.

In Kawi, C_2, the second component of a consonantal conjunct C_1C_2, could be written, in somewhat modified form, under C_1. Thus developed through the medieval period the secondary forms, known as *pasangan* in modern Javanese. Other modifications took place: many letters changed in shape, and several, e.g. those denoting the aspirates, were discarded as irrelevant to the needs of modern Javanese. Punctuation signs were also introduced.

Column 1 in Table 1 shows the primary *aksårå*, column 2 their *pasangan* forms. As noted above, *a* > /ɔ/ is inherent in the aksårå. Table 2 shows the *sandangan* ('clothed') signs used to notate the vowels *e, i, o, u* in post-consonantal position, and certain other phonemes.

In addition, the Classical Javanese script had a series of 'large' or capital letters, for use in the names and titles of distinguished personages.

THE JAVANESE SCRIPT

CONSONANTS

1		2		Name	Value
ꦲ				hå	h (mute)
ꦤ				nå	n
ꦕ				cå	tʃ
ꦫ				rå	r
ꦏ				kå	k (as final > ʔ)
ꦢ				då	d
ꦠ				tå	t
ꦱ				så	s
ꦮ				wå	w
ꦭ				lå	l
ꦥ				på	p
ꦝ				ḍå	ḍ
ꦗ				jå	dʒ
ꦪ				yå	j
ꦚ				ñå	ɲ
ꦩ				må	m
ꦒ				gå	g
ꦧ				bå	b
ꦛ				ṭå	ṭ
ꦔ				ngå	ŋ

Source: Bohatta, H. (n.d.) *Praktische Grammatik der Javanischen Sprache,* Vienna.

VOWELS AND OTHER SYMBOLS

Sign		Name	Value
⌒	∩	pĕpĕt	ĕ
⊃	∩	wulu	i
⌐	⌐	suku	u
⌐	⌐	taling	é/è
⌐⁻₂	η — ₂	taling-tarung	o (circumfix)
⌐	⌐	pangkon Kr., patĕn Ng.	cancels inherent vowel; corresponds to Devanagari virāma
⌐	⌐	pingkal	marks palatalized consonant
⌐,⌐	⌐ (	cåkrå	post-consonantal r
⌐	⌐	kĕrĕt	rĕ following a consonant
/	⁄	layar	syllabic final r
⌐ ·	?	wigūan	syllabic final h
ˑ	ˑ	cĕcak	syllabic final ŋ
⌐	⌐ ⌐ ⌐	pa-cĕrĕk	rĕ
⌐	⌐ ⌐ ⌐	ngå-lĕlĕt	lĕ

Vowels in isolation: these occur mainly in foreign words:

a   e   i

o   u

In the vowel table above, Kr. refers to Krama /krɔmɔ/ 'polite, formal speech'; Ng. refers to Ngoko 'colloquial speech'.

Source: Bohatta, H. (n.d.) *Praktische Grammatik der Javanischen Sprache*, Vienna.

KANNADA

The Kannaḍa (also known as Kanarese) script is a derivative of Brāhmī. Between the Brāhmī source and the Kannada script, as it appears from the fourteenth century onwards, a transitional script was in use which also underlies Telugu (**q.v.**). The table shows the modern Kannada inventory of consonants and vowels: the latter (a) independent (initial only), and (b) as applied to the consonant /k/. As in most Indian scripts, the short vowel /a/ is inherent in each base consonant: thus ಕ is /ka/.

Conjunct consonants are in general formed by subscription of the second component, which is often abbreviated.

THE KANNADA SCRIPT

CONSONANTS

ಕ	ಖ	ಗ	ಘ	ಜ
ka	*kha*	*ga*	*gha*	*nga*
ಚ	ಛ	ಜ	ಝ	ಞ
ca	*cha*	*ja*	*jha*	*nya*
ಟ	ಠ	ಡ	ಢ	ಣ
ṭa	*ṭha*	*ḍa*	*ḍha*	*ṇa*
ತ	ಥ	ದ	ಧ	ನ
ta	*tha*	*da*	*dha*	*na*
ಪ	ಫ	ಬ	ಭ	ಮ
pa	*pha*	*ba*	*bha*	*ma*
ಯ	ರ	ಲ	ವ	
ya	*ra*	*la*	*va*	
ಶ	ಷ	ಸ	ಹ	ಳ
śa	*ṣa*	*sa*	*ha*	*la*

VOWELS

ಅ	ಆ	ಇ	ಈ	ಉ	ಊ	ಋ
a	*ā*	*i*	*ī*	*u*	*ū*	*ru*
ಎ	ಏ	ಐ	ಒ	ಓ	ಔ	
e	*ē*	*ai*	*o*	*ō*	*au*	

Vowel signs: here illustrated as applied to *ka*:

ಕಾ *kā,*   ಕಿ *ki,*   ಕೀ *kī,*   ಕು *ku,*   ಕೂ *kū,*   ಕೃ *kru,*   ಕೆ *ke,*

ಕೇ *kē,*   ಕೈ *kai,*   ಕೊ *ko,*   ಕೋ *kō,*   ಕೌ *kau*

NUMERALS

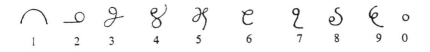

1	2	3	4	5	6	7	8	9	0

KOREAN

Buddhist missionaries from China, and Buddhist texts in Chinese reached Korea around the turn of the millennium, and by the fifth century Korea was a Buddhist state using Chinese as the language of administration and culture. The subsequent spread of Confucianism in the Korean Middle Ages reinforced the status and the use of Chinese. It is not surprising that after nearly two thousand years of unremitting exposure to Chinese influence, well over 50 per cent of Korean vocabulary consists of Chinese borrowings.

By the seventh century, however, scholars were looking for ways of using Chinese characters to notate native Korean words. Among the earliest examples extant are the *hyangga* folksongs. The problem of adapting the morphemic Chinese script to the requirements of a highly inflected, agglutinative language, was being faced at very much the same time in Japan; and, as in the analogous case of Japanese, three possible paths were explored: (a) semantic transfer: a Chinese character was used to denote its Korean semantic equivalent; in a language as heavily sinicized as Korean this must have seemed an attractive solution; (b) phonetic representation: Chinese characters were used to 'spell' Korean words; (c) Chinese characters, functioning as semantic nuclei, were supplied with phonetic diacritics to indicate the additional material (inflections, particles) required by Korean grammar and syntax (cf. the okototen system in Japanese).

A practical solution such as was developed in Japan in the shape of the elegant and tractable wabun script, eluded the Korean scholars. In the middle of the fifteenth century, however, a group of scholars under the aegis and direction of the fourth monarch of the Yi Dynasty, King Sejong (reigned 1418/19–1450) produced the phonetic syllabary of twenty-eight letters known as Hangŭl. Within a year or two of its promulgation, the new script had been used in the poetical work *Yong.pi ŏch'ŏn ka* (Dragon(s) Flying to the Heavens).

The Korean syllabary has been described as 'one of the most scientific alphabets in use in any country' (*Encyclopaedia Britannica*). In fact, however, for the next 400 years, little use was made of it. Chinese remained as before the status language of the educated and influential classes. Of all the written material produced in Korea between the invention of the Hangŭl syllabary and the late nineteenth century, less than 1 per cent is in Korean: the rest is in Chinese.

Towards the end of the nineteenth century, the so-called 'mixed script' began to gain ground. In this system, much as in modern Japanese, Chinese characters function as root morphemes, while the syllabary is used for inflections and particles. Since the late 1940s, use of Chinese characters has been discontinued in North Korea, while in South Korea mixed script continues to be used.

The syllabary is set out in the accompanying tables. The most interesting feature of Hangŭl is the way in which consonants and vowels combine in their base forms to form syllables. That is to say, vowels following consonants do not assume secondary forms as in Devanāgarī, nor are the consonants themselves modified as in Ethiopic. The consonantal inventory takes into account the three-fold division of Korean stops into lax, aspirated and tense. The tense consonants are geminates of the lax: cf. ㄱ /k/, ㄲ /kk/; ㅂ /p/. ㅃ /pp/. To distinguish aspiration the consonant is marked: ㄱ /k/, ㅋ /kʰ/, while palatalization is notated in the vocalic series: 가 /ka/, 갸 /kya/. Vowels cannot stand alone, but must be supported by the bearer ㅇ (not to be confused with the consonantal sign for /n/): thus 아 /a/, 오 /o/.

THE KOREAN SCRIPT

THE SYLLABARY

Letter	*Transcription*	*Letter*	*Transcription*
Pure vowels:			
ㅣ	/i/	ㅡ	/ŭ/
ㅔ	/e/	ㅓ	/ə/
ㅐ	/æ/	ㅏ	/a/
ㅟ	/ü/	ㅜ	/u/
ㅚ	/ö/	ㅗ	/o/
Compound vowels:			
ㅑ	/ya/	ㅘ	/wa
ㅒ	/yæ/	ㅙ	/wæ/
ㅕ	/yə/	ㅝ	/wə/
ㅖ	/ye/	ㅞ	/we/
ㅛ	/yo/	ㅢ	/ŭi/
ㅠ	/yu/		
Consonants:			
ㄱ	/k/	ㅇ	/ŋ/
ㄴ	/n/	ㅈ	/c/
ㄷ	/t/	ㅊ	$/c^h/$
ㄹ	/l/	ㅋ	$/k^h/$
ㅁ	/m/	ㅌ	$/t^h/$
ㅂ	/p/	ㅍ	$/p^h/$
ㅅ	/s/	ㅎ	/h/
Double consonants:			
ㄲ	/k'/	ㅆ	/s'/
ㄸ	/t'/	ㅉ	/c'/
ㅃ	/p'/		

Source: Kim, N. – K. (1987) 'Korean', in B. Comrie (ed.) *The World's Major Languages*, London, Routledge.

Two sample rows follow:

(a) C + V

가	갸	거	겨	고	교	구	규	그
ka	*kya*	*kə*	*kyə*	*ko*	*kyo*	*ku*	*kyu*	*kŭ*

기	걔	걔	게	계	괴	귀	긔	과
ki	*kæ*	*kyæ*	*ke*	*kye*	*ko*	*ki*	*kwi*	*kwa*

궈	괘	궤
kwə	*kwæ*	*kwe*

(b) C + V + C (phonetic realizations)

각	간	간	갈	감	갑	갓	강
kak	*kan*	*kat*	*kal*	*kam*	*kap*	*kat*	*kang*

갗	갖	같	갚	갛	갉	값	갔
kat	*kat*	*kat*	*kap*	*ka'*	*kak*	*kap*	*kat*

LAO

Lao belongs to the south-western group of Tai languages, which also includes Thai, Shan, Yuan, along with many minor languages.

The Lao script, the *tua lao*, dates from about the sixteenth century. Previously, the *tham* (< Pali *dhamma*, Sanskrit *dharma*) script had been used for Buddhist texts in Lao. The tua lao script bears a very close resemblance to Thai, both apparently deriving from a proto-Thai original now lost. The tua lao shares the etymologically motivated but now redundant duplications found in the Thai script.

Lao has six tones. As in Thai, syllabic tone is a function of the following factors:

1. (a)   grade of consonant (high, medium or low);
    (b)   presence of transposing agent ຫ *ho* (cf. Thai ห);

2.   vowel length (short or long);

3.   nature of syllable final:
    (a)   *p, t* or *k*: closed syllable;
    (b)   long vowel or *i/y*: open;
    (c)   *m, n* or *ng*: half-closed;

4.   presence or absence of a tone marker (*mai ek*, *mai to*, etc.; see **Thai**).

THE LAO SCRIPT

CONSONANTS

ກ	ຂ	ຄ	ງ	ຈ	ສ	ຊ
ko	*kho*	*kho*	*ngo*	*cho*	*so*	*so*

ຍ	ດ	ຕ	ຖ	ທ	ນ	ບ
nyo	*do*	*to*	*tho*	*tho*	*no*	*bo*

ປ	ຜ	ຝ	ພ	ຟ	ມ	ຢ
po	*pho*	*fo*	*pho*	*fo*	*mo*	*yo*

ຣ	ລ	ວ	ຫ	ອ	ຮ
ro	*lo*	*wo*	*ho*	*'o*	*ho*

VOWELS

Notation of the rich vocalic system is virtually identical with that of Thai (q.v.), using superscript, subscript, prefixed and suffixed markers, and circumfix. For example, if C represents a consonant, Cາ = Cā, C$_u$ = Cū, Ĉ = Ci, ເĈາ = Cau, ເCາະ = Co, ໂC = Cō.

NUMERALS

໑	໒	໓	໔	໕	໖	໗	໘	໙	໐
1	2	3	4	5	6	7	8	9	0

MALAYALAM

The separation of this Dravidian language (Malayāḷam) from the closely related Tamil (**q.v.**) took place gradually, and relatively recently, in the period from the tenth to the thirteenth century AD. The script now used for Malayalam was introduced in the seventeenth century, and is associated with the illustrious name of Tuñcatt' Eẓuttachan, a key figure in Malayalam literature. Structurally, and especially in the vocalization patterns, the script is largely modelled on Tamil. In contrast with Tamil, however, which reduces the typical Brāhmī-Devanāgarī positional five-term row to two of its members, Malayalam has appropriated the entire grid, even though many of the letters thus generated never figure in Malayalam words.

The basic inventory of consonants and independent vowels is set out in the accompanying table. The table shows the retroflex row as modulated by twelve vowels (short *a* is inherent in the base form of each consonant).

Vocalization patterns for the semi-vowels, sibilants and aspirate are similar.

Conjunct consonants: geminates by duplication, linear or vertical, often with substantial deformation. Conjuncts other than geminates often employ ligatures.

The Arabic numerals are now in general use.

THE MALAYALAM SCRIPT

CONSONANTS

ക	ഖ	ഗ	ഘ	ങ
ka	kha	ga	gha	nga
ച	ഛ	ജ	ഝ	ഞ
ca	cha	ja	jha	nya
ട	ഠ	ഡ	ഢ	ണ
ṭa	ṭha	ḍa	ḍha	ṇa
ത	ഥ	ദ	ധ	ന
ta	tha	da	dha	na
പ	ഫ	ബ	ഭ	മ
pa	pha	ba	bha	ma
യ	ര	ല	വ	
ya	ra	la	va	

ശ	ഷ	സ	ഹ	ള	ഴ	റ
śa	ṣa	sa	ha	ḷa	ṛa	ṟa

VOWELS

(a) independent

അ	ആ	ഇ	ഈ	ഉ	ഊ	ഋ
a	ā	i	ī	u	ū	ru

എ	ഏ	ഐ	ഒ	ഓ	ഔ
e	ē	ai	o	ō	au

(b) as applied to letter ṭa:

ടാ ṭā	ടി ṭi	ടീ ṭī	ടു ṭu	ടൂ ṭū	ടൃ ṭru

ടെ ṭe	ടേ ṭē	ടൈ ṭai	ടൊ ṭo	ടോ ṭō	ടൗ ṭau

MONGOLIAN

The old Mongolian literary language is something of an enigma in that no known form of spoken Mongolian can be conclusively shown to be its basis. When it first appears in the thirteenth century AD, the language is already equipped with a sophisticated writing system and a literary identity, pointing to antecedent development in circumstances that can only be guessed at. The pre-Genghiz Khan Kereits and the Khitans have been seen as possible sources; both of these peoples were in contact with Nestorian Christianity and with Buddhism, and both were on a significantly higher cultural plane than the other Mongolian tribes.

The immediate source of the script itself is certainly the Old Uighur script, which in its turn was based on the Nestorian version of Syriac Estrangelo (see **Syriac**). Uighur retained the horizontal right-to-left format of Syriac, and this format was still being used in the fourteenth century by the Mongol Khans in Persia. In China, however (the Mongol Yuan Dynasty ruled China from 1279 to 1368), when work began on translating the Buddhist scriptures into Mongolian, a vertical format, left to right across the page, was adopted, probably under Chinese influence. As might be expected in view of their Semitic origins, the letters have initial, medial and final forms. From the fifteenth century onwards, eight additional letters were brought into use to notate non-Mongol phonemes occurring in loan-words.

The basic inventory of the Classical Mongolian script is set out in the table. Post-revolutionary writing in Mongolian (1917–40) was exclusively in the classical script. In 1941 Cyrillic was officially adopted for the notation of Khalkha Mongolian. However, the classical script continued to be used for private correspondence etc. by older people in Mongolia, and generally in Inner Mongolia and in Xīnjiāng, where it seems to be still in use.

Even before the Qing (Manchu) Dynasty came to power in China (1644), Manchu scholars had come to know and use the Mongolian script. In 1599, Nurhaci, the founder of the Qing Dynasty, commissioned his chief interpreter, Erdeni, to provide a script for the hitherto unwritten Manchu language. Erdeni was able to adapt the Mongol script to Manchu requirements, a fairly straightforward process, as the two languages are phonologically close to each other. This initial Manchu script was

94

systematized in 1632 by another outstanding linguist, Dahai, who also introduced a method of using diacritical points to distinguish between homographs. Thus, in the earlier script ⼁ could be read as *n*, *a*, or *e*. Dahai restricted ⼁ to *a*, adding a point at the left for *n*: ⼁ and a point at the right for *e*: ⼁.

THE MONGOLIAN SCRIPT

THE ALPHABET

Initial	Medial	Final	Transcription
᠊	᠊	᠊ ᠊	*a*
᠊	᠊	᠊ ᠊	*e*
᠊	᠊	᠊	*i*
᠊	᠊	᠊	*o*
᠊	᠊	᠊	*u*
᠊	᠊ ᠊	᠊	*ö*
᠊	᠊ ᠊	᠊	*ü*
᠊	᠊	᠊ ᠊	*n*
᠊	᠊	᠊	*b*
᠊	᠊	—	*ch*
᠊	᠊	—	*gh*
᠊	᠊	᠊ ᠊	*k*
᠊	᠊	—	*g*
᠊	᠊	᠊	*m*
᠊	᠊	᠊	*l*
᠊	᠊	᠊	*r*

Initial	Medial	Final	Transcription
ọ	◁ ◁	⏊	t
ọ	◁	—	d
◁	◁	—	y
◁	∪	—	j, ds
∪	∪	—	ts
⇀	⇁	⇝	s
⇀,	⇁,	—	š
◁	◁	—	w

Important ligatures are:

Initial	Medial	Final	Transcription
∄	∄	⅀	ai
∄	∄	⅀	oi

Final	Medial
℔ *ba, be*	♇ *bi* ♧ *bo, bu*
↷ *ke, ge*	↗ *ki, gi* ⌆ { *kö, kü* / *gö, gü* }
↲ *ng*	

ORIYA

This derivative of Brāhmī, which is used for writing the Oriya (also known as Oḍrī) language (belonging to the Eastern group of New Indo-Aryan languages) makes its first appearance in the fourteenth/fifteenth centuries. The order of letters follows the Devanāgarī model, but in place of the horizontal stroke above each letter, typical of most other Brāhmī derivatives, Oriya uses a curved line. This practice seems to have arisen in the days when Oriya was written on palm-leaves, whose surface was less likely to be damaged by curved strokes.

The chart shows the consonantal inventory of Oriya, along with the independent vowels, the secondary vowel signs in combination with /ga/, and the numerals. As in all New Indo-Aryan languages and Sanskrit, the short vowel /a/ is inherent in the base form of the consonant. In Oriya /a/ is realized as /ɔ/.

Conjunct consonants in Oriya are numerous and unpredictable, individual components being often substantially transformed in combination.

THE ORIYA SCRIPT

The horizontal line drawn over letters in Devanāgarī is replaced in Oriya by a curved line.

CONSONANTS

କ	ଖ	ଗ	ଘ	ଙ
ka	kha	ga	gha	nga
ଚ	ଛ	ଜ	ଝ	ଞ
ca	cha	ja	jha	nya
ଟ	ଠ	ଡ	ଢ	ଣ
ṭa	ṭha	ḍa	ḍha	ṇa
ତ	ଥ	ଦ	ଧ	ନ
ta	tha	da	dha	na
ପ	ଫ	ବ	ଭ	ମ
pa	pha	ba	bha	ma
ଯ	ର	ଳ	ଲ	ଵ
(ja)	ra	la	ḷa	wa
ଶ	ଷ	ସ	ହ	କ୍ଷ
śa	ṣa	sa	ha	khya

VOWELS

(a) independent:

ଅ	ଆ	ଇ	ଈ	ଉ	ଊ	ଋ	ୠ
a	ā	i	ī	u	ū	ru	rū

ଌ	ଏ	ଐ	ଓ	ଔ	ଅଂ	ଅଃ	
lu	ē	ai	ō	au	aṅ	a'	

(b) the secondary vowel signs, used in combination with consonants, are closely similar to the Devanagari series. As illustration, they are here shown with the consonant *ga*:

ଗା   ଗି   ଗୀ   ଗୁ   ଗୂ   ଗୃ
gā   *gi*   *gī*   *gu*   *gū*   *gru*

ଗେ   ଗୈ   ଗୋ   ଗୌ
gē   *gai*   *gō*   *gau*

There are several irregularities in the use of these signs, particularly as regards the notation of *i*, *ī*, and *u*.

NUMERALS

୧	୨	୩	୪	୫	୬	୭	୮	୯	୦
1	2	3	4	5	6	7	8	9	0

ROMAN

Southern Italy and Sicily were colonized by the Greeks in the course of the eighth to the sixth centuries BC; and it was for long assumed that the Latin alphabet was a product of direct contact between Romans and Greeks. However, it is now generally accepted that the link between the two scripts is provided by Etruscan. The Etruscans appear in history about 900 BC. Their period of greatest political, economic and ideological power covered the eighth to the sixth centuries. The following centuries saw a gradual decline in their influence, though the Etruscan city-states were not finally absorbed into the Roman Empire until the first century BC. The language ceased to be used for sacral purposes at about the same time. There is no way of knowing how long it survived as a spoken language.

In spite of repeated efforts to link Etruscan with Indo-European, with agglutinative languages of the Uralic type and with Caucasian languages, no definite relationship with any other language family has ever been established. What is clear is that by about 700 BC the Etruscans were using a Western Greek script to write inscriptions in their language. This early script, as found, for example, in the Marsiliana Tablet (eighth century BC), is a close copy of the original Semito-Greek alphabet (see **Greek**) running from right to left. This script is shown in the left-hand column of Table 1.

The second column of Table 1 shows the classical Etruscan script, now reduced from twenty-six to twenty letters, including the vowels /a, e, i, u/. The earlier script had separate letters for ⅃ and Ọ. These were gradually phased out, and replaced by /c/ = /k/.

The celebrated Praeneste Fibula, preserved in the Luigi Pigorini museum in Rome, shows that by the seventh century BC the Etruscan alphabet was being used to write Latin. In Table 2 early and classical forms of the Etruscan script, as used for Latin, are set out.

It will be seen that the three Greek aspirates, theta, phi and khi, have been discarded as irrelevant to Latin. X and G were added in the third century BC, Y and Z in the first. A thousand years passed before the letters J, U and W were added. Table 3 shows the upright and italic forms of the contemporary script. In the first millennium AD the following types of letters were used for Latin:

square capitals: these have remained virtually unchanged over two millennia;
rustic capitals: first to sixth century;
uncials: a rounded script used from the fourth to the eighth century;
half-uncial: partly cursive.

From the uncials various cursives developed. One of the best-known, certainly one of the most aesthetically pleasing, is the ninth-century Carolingian minuscule (see the illustration on page 109, which also shows two lines – 5 and 6 – in rustic capitals, and one – 7 – in uncial). This Carolingian script, as reinstated by Italian humanists of the fifteenth century, became the model for early printed books in Western Europe, apart from Germany, where a so-called Gothic character became the norm.

Ligatures had proliferated in the book-hands of the Middle Ages before the advent of printing: the sole survivor in modern usage is the ampersand &.

As the natural medium for the Latin language, the Roman script spread by natural diffusion to the educated classes throughout the vast expanses of the Roman Empire: even the hundreds of Berber inscriptions which have been found in Libya are in Roman script (only two, found in the Roman city of Dugga in Tunisia, are in *tifinagh*: see **Berber**).

Problems arose when this lucid but limited script was called upon to cope with emergent national languages like Czech and Hungarian, and, later, when it was extended by missionary activity to hundreds of hitherto unwritten languages. Alien phonemes and phonemic contrasts, both qualitative and quantitative, had to be identified and suitably notated. The Roman script could be usefully expanded in several ways:

1. By using diacritics such as the acute, the grave, the circumflex, the macron, the inverted circumflex, the dot, the umlaut, the tilde and the cedilla.

   The acute accent: some examples of its use:

   (a) used to mark long vowels in Hungarian: *ház* 'house' (here, /aː/ differs not only quantitatively but also qualitatively from short [a] which is /ɑ/);

   (b) marks /e/ in opposition to /ɛ/ in French: *été* 'summer';

(c)   distinguishes homonyms: cf. Spanish, where the acute accent distinguishes the interrogative adverb *cuándo* from the conjunction *cuando*;

(d)   as abnormal or specific stress marker: Spanish, *sábado* 'Saturday';

(e)   marks soft palatalization in Polish: *ć, ń, ś, ź*.

The grave accent:

(a)   in French, used (not exclusively or consistently) to mark /ɛ/: *mère* 'mother';

(b)   in Italian to mark specific accentuation: *città* 'city, town';

(c)   in Bambara, *è* and *ò* are used to denote /ɛ/ and /ɔ/.

The circumflex:

(a)   marks the long vowel /ɛ:/: *sê* 'to say', in Afrikaans;

(b)   marks /o:/ and /ɛ:/ in French etyma with historical presence of /s/: *hôte, bête*;

(c)   in Romanian, marks tense, unrounded /ɨ/: *sînt* 'am', *România* 'Romania'.

The macron: e.g. marks long vowels in Latvian: *ēst* 'to eat', *jūra* 'sea'.

The inverted circumflex (haček) e.g. marks fricatives and affricates in Czech, Lithuanian, Latvian, etc.: *š* = /ʃ/, *č* = /tʃ/: also Czech /ɲ/.

The dot: e.g. in Yoruba, /ɛ/ and /ɔ/ are marked as *ẹ* and *ọ*.

The tilde: In Portuguese, the tilde denotes nasalization: *nações* /nɐsõjʃ/ 'nations'; *mãe* /mɐ̃j/ 'mother'. In Estonian, *õ* denotes the tense unrounded /ɨ/: *õhtu* /ɨhtu/ 'evening'. Spanish and Maasai use *ñ* to denote /ɲ/.

The cedilla: used in French and Portuguese to denote a soft sibilant before a back vowel: Fr. *leçon*, Ptg. *nações*. Polish uses the cedilla to mark nasalization of [a] and [e]: *ząb* /zõb/, pl. *zęba* /zɛ̃ba/ 'tooth, teeth'. A hook is used for nasalization in Navajo: *łį́į́*, 'horse'. In Latvian, *k, l, n, t* are palatalized by cedilla: *ķ, ļ, ņ, ţ*. The cedilla is used in Romanian to denote /ʃ/ *ş* and /ts/ *ţ*.

The umlaut: In German, Hungarian, Finnish, Estonian etc. short /œ/ and /y/ are denoted by *ö* and *ü*. In Hungarian, the long correlatives are marked as *ő*, *ű*. ä /ɛ/ is used in German, Finnish and Estonian.

The apostrophe: used in Czech and Slovak to mark palatalization before back vowels: *t', d'.*

Other diacritics: for /ɔ:/ in Scandinavian languages *å* is used. *ğ* in Latvian denotes palatalized /gj/ tending to /dj/. In Turkish, *ğ* serves mainly to lengthen a preceding back vowel: *dağ* /da:/ 'mountain'.

2. By introducing new letters: e.g. in Danish, Norwegian and Faeroese, *æ*, *ø*, representing /ɛ/ and /œ/. In Icelandic, *þ*, *ð* representing /θ, ð/. Akan, Mende, Kpelle, etc. have introduced *ε*, *ɔ*. In Maltese, *ħ* = Arabic ح ; *għ* = Arabic غ . Turkish uses the undotted ı as the back vowel harmonic corresponding to front /i/. Three new letters appear in Vietnamese: *o'*, *u'*, and *đ* = /d/; (unbarred *d* = /z/).

3. By giving new values to available Roman letters: unbarred *d* = /z/ in Vietnamese has already been mentioned. In Albanian, *x* = /dz/, *xh* = /dʒ/. In Somali, *C* is used to denote the voiced pharyngeal fricative /ʕ/, Arabic ع .

4. By using diacritics as tone markers: for example, the Vietnamese system as applied to the syllable *ma*:

> *má* high rising
>
> *mà* low falling
>
> *mả* low rising
>
> *mã* high broken
>
> *mạ* low broken

In Navajo, the acute accent is used to mark the high tone: *diné* 'man, people'.

Chinese: the official pin-yin romanization marks the four tones of Modern Standard Chinese by means of diacritics: macron for first (high level) tone; acute for second (sharp rising); inverted circumflex for third (long falling–rising); grave for fourth (sharp falling); cf. *mā* 'mother', *má* 'hemp', *mǎ* 'horse', *mà* 'to scold, curse'. Atonic syllables are unmarked: *nǐmen* 'you' (pl.).

5.   For the notation of non-pulmonic sounds (clicks): to denote the ingressive series – the clicks – found in the Khoisan languages, for example, specific sets of symbols have had to be devised. Thus, in !Kung, the dental click is denoted by ǀ, the palatal by !, the alveolar by ǂ and the nasal by ǁ. In Nama, the abrupt gingival stop is marked by ǂ, the correlative affricate by /, the post-alveolar stop by ! and the affricate by //.

THE EARLY WESTERN GREEK AND ETRUSCAN SCRIPTS

Western Greek	Etruscan	
A	A	a
𝈜		b
⌐	⟩	c (k)
⌐		d
Ⅎ	Ⅎ	e
Ⅎ	Ⅎ	v
I	I	z
🄱	🄱 𝈨 𝈩	h
⊗	⊙ ○	th
			i
⅄	⅄	k
↲	↲	l
⋎	⋔ ⋔	m
⅄	⋔ ⋔	n
⊞		s
○		o
⌐	⌐	p
M	M (⌇)	s
Ϙ		q (k)
⊲	⊲	r
⟨	⟨ ⟩	s
T	T ⟙	t
Y	V	u
X		s
Φ		ph
Ψ	Ψ	kh
	8 8	f

Source: Pfiffig, A.J. (1969) *Die Etruskische Sprache*, Graz.

THE ETRUSCAN SCRIPT
AS USED FOR LATIN

A	ʌ ʌ ƌ	A
	B	B
	⟨	C
ꟼ	D	D
ꓞ	ʓ	E
ꓞ	ꓮ	F
		G
ᗊ	H	H
ı	ı	I
ʎ	K	K
	⋁	L
ᴎ	ᴍ	M
Ɥ	ᴎ	N
o	o	O
⌐	⌐	P
	ϙ	Q
	ꓝ	R
ϟ	ϟ	S
	⊤	T
⋁	⋁	V
	×	X
		Y
		Z

Source: *Encyclopaedia Britannica*, 15th edn, 1974.

THE ROMAN ALPHABET

A	B	C	D	E	F	G	H	I	J	K	L	M	N	O	P
a	b	c	d	e	f	g	h	i	j	k	l	m	n	o	p

A	*B*	*C*	*D*	*E*	*F*	*G*	*H*	*I*	*J*	*K*	*L*	*M*	*N*	*O*	*P*
a	*b*	*c*	*d*	*e*	*f*	*g*	*h*	*i*	*j*	*k*	*l*	*m*	*n*	*o*	*p*

Q	R	S	T	U	V	W	X	Y	Z
q	r	s	t	u	v	w	x	y	z

Q	*R*	*S*	*T*	*U*	*V*	*W*	*X*	*Y*	*Z*
q	*r*	*s*	*t*	*u*	*v*	*w*	*x*	*y*	*z*

Source: Galbraith, V.H. (1962) *The Historian at Work,* London, BBC, Plate XIX.

SAMARITAN

A member of the Semito-Hamitic branch of the Afro-Asiatic family of languages, Samaritan was a written and spoken form of Western Aramaic. Three stages may be distinguished in the development of the language:

1. Fourth century BC to eighth century AD; in this oldest period Samaritan was both a spoken and a written language. Samaritan translation of the Targum.

2. Ninth to twelfth century; medieval period; spoken Samaritan ousted by Arabic though the language continued to be written.

3. Thirteenth century onwards: Samaritan no longer spoken; growth of a hybrid literary language, influenced by both Hebrew and Arabic.

The script, shown in the accompanying table, is consonantal, and very close to its Phoenician original. As in Hebrew and Arabic *y* and *w*, function as *matres lectionis* for /iː/ and /uː/.

Certain diacritics accompanying individual words in Samaritan manuscripts have been construed as short-vowel markers; thus, P. Kahle identified | as /a/, < as /i, e/, ∧ as /u, o/. This interpretation is not universally accepted.

THE SAMARITAN SCRIPT

THE ALPHABET

Column 1: square form; column 2: cursive; column 3; transliteration; column 4: phonetic value.

1	2	3	4	1	2	3	4
N	N	'	Ø, '	2	<	l	l, ł
9	9	b	b	3	r	m	m
ͳ	ͳ	g	g	5	3	n	n
٩	٢	d	d	ß	ß	s	s
3	3	h	'	▽	◁	ʿ	ʿ, ', Ø
✗	✗	w	w, b, u	ᴔ	ﻝ	f	f
3	3	z	z	ᵯ	ᵯ	ṣ	ṣ
☆	☆	ḥ	ʿ, ', Ø	☆	7	q	q
ᶹ	ᶹ	ṭ	ł	9	9	r	r
𝑚	𝑚	y	j	ᴊ	ᴊ	š	ʃ
𝄐	𝄐	k	k	N	N	t	t

Source: Vil'sker, L. (1974) *Samaritanskij jazyk*, Moscow.

SINHALESE

Sinhalese (Sinhala) is a New Indo-Aryan language, and it is natural that the oldest Sinhalese inscriptions (dating from the third century BC) should be written in a script which is close to the Asokan Edict script of northern India. In the tenth/eleventh century AD, however, Tamil incursion into Ceylon brought with it a south Indian Grantha-based script (see **Tamil**), and it is this script which has been ever since, and still is, used for Sinhalese.

The table shows the basic consonantal inventory of Sinhalese, along with the independent vowels (used as initials and after other vowels). It should be noted that the original distinction between aspirate and non-aspirate, e.g. *ka/kha*, *ga/gha*, is not relevant in modern Sinhalese, where [ka] = [kha] = /ka/. The aspirates are, of course, written where they are etymologically appropriate, e.g. in Sanskrit and Pali loan-words.

The table also shows the secondary forms of the vowels as applied to the consonants *na*. As in all Indian scripts, each base consonant has an inherent vowel. In Sinhalese this vowel is /a/ or /ə/ depending on syllable position.

Conjunct consonants: the subscript model as used in Telugu and Malayalam is not found in Sinhalese. Instead, there is an extensive repertory of ligatures, many of which are of great complexity, particularly those representing combinations found in Pali and Sanskrit loan-words.

Ligatures may be replaced by writing the two components separately.

THE SINHALESE SCRIPT

CONSONANTS

ක	බ	ග	ඝ	ඞ
ka	kha	ga	gha	nga
ච	ඡ	ජ	ඣ	ඤ
ca	cha	ja	jha	nya
ට	ඨ	ඩ	ඪ	ණ
ṭa	ṭha	ḍa	ḍha	ṇa
ත	ථ	ද	ධ	න
ta	tha	da	dha	na
ප	ඵ	බ	භ	ම
pa	pha	ba	bha	ma
ය	ර	ල	ව	
ya	ra	la	va	
ශ	ෂ	ස	හ	ළ
śa	ṣa	sa	ha	la

VOWELS

Independent:

අ	ආ	ඇ	ඈ	ඉ	ඊ	උ	ඌ
a	ā	æ	ǣ	i	ī	u	ū
සෘ	එ	ඒ	ඓ	ඔ	ඕ	ඖ	
ri	e	ē	ai	o	ō	au	

The vowels as applied to the consonant na

නා	නැ	නෑ	නි	නී	නු	නූ
nā	næ	nǣ	ni	nī	nu	nū
නෘ	නෙ	නේ	නෛ	නො	නෝ	නෞ
nri	ne	nē	nai	no	nō	nau

The Arabic numerals are now in general use.

SYRIAC

This North-West Semitic language, centring on the Mesopotamian city of Edessa (present-day Urfa in Turkey) was one of the most important derivatives of literary Aramaic. The oldest inscriptions in what is recognizably Syriac go back to the turn of the millennia. From the third to the seventh century, Syriac was the medium for a rich and important Christian literature, comprising both original writing and translation from Greek. The Syriac Vulgate is represented by the *peshitta*, i.e. 'simple', redaction of the Old Syriac translation of the New Testament. The peshitta was more or less complete by the end of the fourth century.

Until the fifth century Syriac was written in the consonantal Estrangelo/ Estrangela script (< Greek στρογγυλὴ 'circular'), in which the letters ālaph, yud and vau were used as *matres lectionis* to denote the long vowels *ā, ī, ū* (cf. **Hebrew**). Table 1 shows the Estrangelo consonantal alphabet.

Following the Council of Edessa (431) two successor writing systems took shape, neither of them differing to any great extent from Estrangelo. The Eastern Syrians in the Persian Empire adopted the Nestorian variant, with pointing on the Hebrew model, while the Western (Jacobite) church opted for the so-called *serṭo* ('line') script, with inverted-reversed Greek letters acting as vowel markers: see Table 2.

Daghesh (see **Hebrew**): theoretically, in Syriac, the daghesh point which marks *b, g, d, k, p* or *t* as a stop, is placed above the letter; placed under the letter, the point marks the correlative spirant. However, there is no consistency, and the rule is generally disregarded.

A point placed under a verbal initial was frequently used to indicate the perfective aspect. Two points (known as *ribui*) may be placed over a word to indicate the plural number.

A short line drawn over or under a consonant indicates that it is mute.

THE SYRIAC SCRIPT

THE CONSONANTAL ALPHABET

Separate		Joined	Name	Hebrew		English
	ܐ	ܠܠܐ	Ālaph	א		'
ܩ	ܩ	ܩܩܩ	Beth	ב		b, bh (v)
ܓ	ܓ	ܓܓܓ	Gāmal	ג		g, gh
	ܕ	ܕܕ	Dālath	ד		d, dh
	ܗ	ܗܗܗ	He	ה		h
	ܘ	ܘܘܘ	Vau	ו		v or w
	ܙ	ܙܠܠ	Zain	ז		z
ܚ	ܚ	ܚܚܚ	Ḥeth	ח		ḥ
ܛ	ܛ	ܛܛܛ	Ṭeth	ט		ṭ
ܝ	ܝ	ܝܝܝ	Yud	י		y in yet
ܟ	ܟ	ܟܟܟ	Kāph	ך כ		k, kh
ܠ	ܠ	ܠܠ	Lāmad	ל		l
ܡ	ܡ	ܡܡܡ	Mim	ם מ		m
ܢ	ܢ	ܢܢ	Nun	ן נ		n
ܤ	ܤ	ܤܤܤ	Semkath	ס		s
ܥ	ܥ	ܥܥܥ	'Ē	ע		'
ܦ	ܦ	ܦܦܦ	Pe	ף פ		p, ph
ܨ	ܨ	ܨܨ	Tsāde	ץ צ		ts
ܩ	ܩ	ܩܩܩ	Ḳuph	ק		ḳ
ܪ	ܪ	ܪܪܪ	Rish	ר		r
ܫ	ܫ	ܫܫܫ	Shin	ש		sh
	ܬ	ܬܬ	Thau	ת		t, th

Source: *Elements of Syriac Grammar*, London, Bagster (n. d.).

THE VOWELS

Vowel	Jacobite notation	Nestorian notation
a	⅂	،
ā	⌒	، ،
e	⌒ or ⌒	، ،
i	⊏ or ⊏	،
o.u	⋏	Oˈ
ō.ū	⋏	O،

TAMIL

The Tamil syllabary derives, via Grantha forms, from the Brāhmī script. The grid consists of eighteen consonants (each with inherent /a/) and twelve vowels (including two diphthongs, /ai/ and /au/). See the accompanying table. Traditionally, the consonants are known as 'body-letters' and the vowels as 'life-letters'; the vocalized consonants are then known as 'life–body letters' or 'animated forms'.

From the table it will be seen that the typical Brāhmī–Devanāgarī positional row is reduced in Tamil to its first and last members, i.e. the unvoiced non-aspirate and the homorganic nasal: e.g. for the velar row, [k] and [ṅ]. This means that positionally determined allophones have to share one and the same graph with their base consonant. Thus, க /ka/ also represents /ga/ (following nasals), /x/ (in non-initial syllables if not preceded by க, ட, or a nasal) and the aspirates /kha, gha, h/ (in Sanskrit loan-words). Similarly ச represents /tʃ]/, dʒ/ and /s/.

Five Grantha letters are used in Sanskrit words for /ja – ṣa – sa – ha – kṣa/. Use of these Grantha letters may depend on register, i.e. whether formal or everyday language is being used.

Inherent /a/ is cancelled by a superscript dot.

The Arabic and Roman numerals are now standard. Punctuation is as in English.

THE TAMIL SCRIPT

THE SYLLABARY

—		அ a	ஆ ā	இ i	ஈ ī	உ u	ஊ ū
க்	k	க ka	கா kā	கி ki	கீ kī	கு ku	கூ kū
ங்	ṅ	ங ṅa	ஙா ṅā	ஙி ṅi	ஙீ ṅī	ஙு ṅu	ஙூ ṅū
ச்	ç	ச ça	சா çā	சி çi	சீ çī	சு çu	சூ çū
ஞ்	ñ	ஞ ña	ஞா ñā	ஞி ñi	ஞீ ñī	ஞு ñu	ஞூ ñū
ட்	ḍ	ட ḍa	டா ḍā	டி ḍi	டீ ḍī	டு ḍu	டூ ḍū
ண்	ṇ	ண ṇa	ணா ṇā	ணி ṇi	ணீ ṇī	ணு ṇu	ணூ ṇū
த்	t	த ta	தா tā	தி ti	தீ tī	து tu	தூ tū
ந்	n	ந na	நா nā	நி ni	நீ nī	நு nu	நூ nū
ப்	p	ப pa	பா pā	பி pi	பீ pī	பு pu	பூ pū
ம்	m	ம ma	மா mā	மி mi	மீ mī	மு mu	மூ mū
ய்	y	ய ya	யா yā	யி yi	யீ yī	யு yu	யூ yū
ர்	r	ர ra	ரா rā	ரி ri	ரீ rī	ரு ru	ரூ rū
ல்	l	ல la	லா lā	லி li	லீ lī	லு lu	லூ lū
வ்	v	வ va	வா vā	வி vi	வீ vī	வு vu	வூ vū
ழ்	ẓ	ழ ẓa	ழா ẓā	ழி ẓi	ழீ ẓī	ழு ẓu	ழூ ẓū
ள்	ḷ	ள ḷa	ளா ḷā	ளி ḷi	ளீ ḷī	ளு ḷu	ளூ ḷū
ற்	R	ற Ra	றா Rā	றி Ri	றீ Rī	று Ru	றூ Rū
ன்	N	ன Na	னா Nā	னி Ni	னீ Nī	னு Nu	னூ Nū

எ	e	ஏ	ē	ஐ	ai	ஒ	o	ஓ	ō	ஔ	au
கெ	ke	கே	kē	கை	kai	கொ	ko	கோ	kō	கௌ	kau
ஙெ	ṅe	ஙே	ṅē	ஙை	ṅai	ஙொ	ṅo	ஙோ	ṅō	ஙௌ	ṅau
செ	çe	சே	çē	சை	çai	சொ	ço	சோ	çō	சௌ	çau
ஞெ	ñe	ஞே	ñē	ஞை	ñai	ஞொ	ño	ஞோ	ñō	ஞௌ	ñau
டெ	ḍe	டே	ḍē	டை	ḍai	டொ	ḍo	டோ	ḍō	டௌ	ḍau
ணெ	ṇe	ணே	ṇē	ணை	ṇai	ணொ	ṇo	ணோ	ṇō	ணௌ	ṇau
தெ	te	தே	tē	தை	tai	தொ	to	தோ	tō	தௌ	tau
நெ	ne	நே	nē	நை	nai	நொ	no	நோ	nō	நௌ	nau
பெ	pe	பே	pē	பை	pai	பொ	po	போ	pō	பௌ	pau
மெ	me	மே	mē	மை	mai	மொ	mo	மோ	mō	மௌ	mau
யெ	ye	யே	yē	யை	yai	யொ	yo	யோ	yō	யௌ	yau
ரெ	re	ரே	rē	ரை	rai	ரொ	ro	ரோ	rō	ரௌ	rau
லெ	le	லே	lē	லை	lai	லொ	lo	லோ	lō	லௌ	lau
வெ	ve	வே	vē	வை	vai	வொ	vo	வோ	vō	வௌ	vau
ழெ	ẓe	ழே	ẓē	ழை	ẓai	ழொ	ẓo	ழோ	ẓō	ழௌ	ẓau
ளெ	ḷe	ளே	ḷē	ளை	ḷai	ளொ	ḷo	ளோ	ḷō	ளௌ	ḷau
றெ	Re	றே	Rē	றை	Rai	றொ	Ro	றோ	Rō	றௌ	Rau
னெ	Ne	னே	Nē	னை	Nai	னொ	No	னோ	Nō	னௌ	Nau

Source: Steever, S.B. (1987) 'Tamil and the Dravidian Languages', in B. Comrie (ed.) *The World's Major Languages*, London, Routledge, adapted from Pope, G.U. (1979) *A Handbook of the Tamil Language*, New Delhi, Asian Education Services.

TELUGU

The Telugu script derives from Brāhmī via a transitional Grantha character, which was, until the fourteenth century, also used for writing Kannada (**q.v.**). Even after separating, the Telugu and Kannada syllabaries remain very close to each other. The table shows the full Telugu inventory of thirty-four consonants, as set out in the traditional Devanāgarī (**q.v.**) order. However, in modern Telugu the ten aspirated consonants are found in only a few Sanskrit loan-words, while *nga* and *nya* are also rare. The great majority of Telugu words can be written in terms of the remaining twenty-two consonants, plus O the polyvalent sign for nasalization (anusvāra).

Surprisingly, the vowel inventory includes no graph for the important phoneme /æ/ which acts, *inter alia*, as a past-tense marker; cf. *waccæ:du* 'he came', *cadivæ:du* 'he read'. In the official orthography, *a:* is generally used to denote the missing *æ*. The base from inherent vowel is /a/.

Conjunct consonants in Telugu are mostly geminates, the second component being subscribed in primary or secondary form.

THE TELUGU SCRIPT

CONSONANTS

క	ఖ	గ	ఘ	జ
ka	kha	ga	gha	nga
చ	ఛ	జ	ఝ	ఞ
ca	cha	ja	jha	nya
ట	ఠ	డ	ఢ	ణ
ṭa	ṭha	ḍa	ḍha	ṇa
త	థ	ద	ధ	న
ta	tha	da	dha	na
ప	ఫ	బ	భ	మ
pa	pha	ba	bha	ma
య	ర	ల	ళ	వ
ya	ra	la	ḷa	va
శ	ష	స	హ	
śa	ṣa	sa	ha	

VOWELS

(a) independent:

అ	ఆ	ఇ	ఈ	ఉ	ఊ	ఋ
a	ā	i	ī	u	ū	ru
ఎ	ఏ	ఐ	ఒ	ఓ	ఔ	
e	ē	ai	o	ō	au	

(b) as applied to the consonant *ka*:

కా	కి	కీ	కు	కూ	కృ
kā	ki	kī	ku	kū	kru
కె	కే	కై	కొ	కో	కౌ
ke	kē	kai	ko	kō	kau

There are many irregularities.

NUMERALS

౧	౨	౩	౪	౫	౬	౭	౮	౯	౦
1	2	3	4	5	6	7	8	9	0

THAI

The Thai script, dating from the late thirteenth century, seems to have been borrowed in part from the Khmer version of a south Indian script. It has no ligatures. The short vowel /ɔ/ is inherent in the base form of each consonant. The degree of redundancy is high, with five graphs for /kh/, six for /th/ and four for /s/, etymologically explicable but no longer phonologically justifiable.

The table shows the Thai inventory of consonants representing the five positional series originally present in the Indian source. It will be seen that forty-four letters are used to notate twenty-one consonantal phonemes; a further fourteen symbols serve, single and in combination, to denote over thirty vowel sounds. There are no capital letters. Words in connected text are not separated from each other by spaces.

As will be seen from the table, the Thai consonants are divided into three classes: high, middle and low. This division is in part phonological in that the unaspirated consonants are grouped as middle-class, the aspirates as high- or low-class.

The table also shows the vocalization system as applied to the low-class consonant /kh/. Thai has no forms for independent vowels. Seven collinear symbols: ไ, ะ, เ, แ, โ, ใ, ไ, five superscripts: ◌ ◌ ◌ ◌ ◌, and two subscripts ◌ , ◌ combine with each other and with the consonants ง, ย, อ, to generate the vowel system. Some combinations are very rare. Permissible consonantal finals are the nasals and *p*, *t*, *k*. Final *p*, *t*, *k* are not fully released. In final position, the affricates and the sibilants are all realized as Thai /d/. Cf. *samrej* > /samred/ 'accomplished', *angris* > /angrid/ 'English', *prathes* > /prathed/ 'country'.

ORTHOGRAPHY AND TONE

(a)   Without tone mark

1.   Low- or middle-class initial; final is not *k*, *t* or *p*: *common* tone, e.g.

มา *ma* 'to come'

เรียน *rian* 'to learn'

2.   high-class initial; final is not *k*, *t* or *p*: *rising* tone, e.g.

สอง *sɔ̌ng* 'two'

3.   low-class initial plus short vowel plus *k*, *t* or *p* final: *high* tone, e.g.

นัก *nak* 'very'

4.   low-class initial plus long vowel plus *k*, *t* or *p* final: *falling* tone, e.g.

มาก *mâk* 'much, many'

5.   high- or middle-class initial plus short or long vowel plus *k*, *t* or *p* final: *low* tone, e.g.

ปวด *buat* 'to ache'

6.   low-class initial plus short open vowel: *high* tone, e.g.

และ *lɛ̌'* 'and'

7.   high- or middle-class initial plus short open vowel: *low* tone, e.g.

จะ *ca'* (future marker)

(b)   With tone mark

mai-ek ': changes tone of syllable with middle- or high-class initial to low tone, irrespective of ending:

ส่ง *song* 'to send';

mai-to ย: changes tone of syllable with middle- or high-class initial, irrespective of ending, to falling:

ห้า *ha* 'five'

also changes tone of syllable with low-class initial to high tone:

ม้า *ma* 'horse'

น้ำ *nam* 'water'.

Two further tone markers are found in a very few words: *maitri* ◌ and *maicadtawā* ◌. The former raises a syllable with a middle-class initial to a high tone; the latter gives such a syllable a rising tone.

Other signs used in the Thai script:

(a)   ๆ : this sign marks repetition of a syllable: บ่อย ๆ *bɔjbɔj* 'often'.

(b)   ◌ : this superscript sign marks its bearer consonant as mute: cf.

เสาร์ *sow* 'Saturday'

(c)   ๆ marks abbreviation; for example, the very lengthy (155 letters) full name of Bangkok is abbreviated to กรุงเทพ ๆ *grungthep*.

(d)   ◌ : this superscript sign shortens the vowel sound marked by เ (rarely by แ) followed by a consonant: cf. เห็น *hen* 'to see', เป็น *ben* 'to be'. ◌ is not used when a tone mark is present. Note, however, that a tone mark itself often shortens the relevant vowel: cf. เล่น *len* (falling tone, shortened) 'to play'.

THE THAI SCRIPT

CONSONANTS

Mid	Mid	High	High	Low	Low	Low	Low
	ก	ข	ฃ	ค	ฅ	ฆ	ง
	k	kh	kh	kh	kh	kh	ng
	จ	ฉ		ช	ซ	ฌ	ญ
	c	ch		ch	s	ch	y
ฎ	ฏ	ฐ		ฑ		ฒ	ณ
d	t	th		th		th	n
ด	ต	ถ		ท		ธ	น
d	t	th		th		th	n
บ	ป	ผ	ฝ	พ	ฟ	ภ	ม
b	p	ph	f	ph	f	ph	m

The sixth group in Devanāgarī, comprising the semi-vowels, and the spirants, is represented in Thai as follows:

(a) the semi-vowels (all low class consonants):

ย	ร	ล	ว
y	r	l	w

(b) the spirants (all high class consonants):

ศ	ษ	ส
s	s	s

(c) the mixed group ห h (high), ฬ l (low), อ ? (middle), ฮ h (low).

NUMERALS

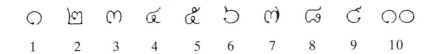

๑	๒	๓	๔	๕	๖	๗	๘	๙	๑๐
1	2	3	4	5	6	7	8	9	10

VOWELS

	Long With final		Long Without final	Short With final				Short Without final
	y	Other		y	w	m	Other	
a		คา		ไค ใค	เคา	คำ	คัน	คะ ค
ə	เคย	เคิน	เคอ					เคอะ
e		เค			เค็น			เคะ
o		โค			คน			โคะ
ua	ควน		คัว		*			คัวะ
ia		เคีย			*			เคียะ
ɨa		เคือ			*			เคือะ
ɛ		แค			แค็น			แคะ
		คอ			คอน			เคาะ
ɨ		คืน	คือ		คึ			
i		คี			คิ			
u		คู			คุ			

Source: Hudak, T.J. (1987) 'Thai', in B. Comrie (ed.) *The World's Major Languages*, London, Routledge, adapted from Brown, J.M. (1967) *A.U.A Center Thai Course*, vol. 3, Bangkok, Social Science Association Press of Thailand, pp. 211–12.

TIBETAN

Tibetan belongs to the Bodish branch of the Sino-Tibetan family of languages. The ethnonym is *bod.pa* (whence Bodish), pronounced as /poe.pa/. The literary language dates from the seventh century AD, when Buddhism began to penetrate into Tibet. As a necessary first step towards the translation of the Buddhist scriptures into Tibetan, King Srong.brTSan.sGam.po commissioned a group of scholars to study Indian writing systems with a view to finding a script for Tibetan. Brāhmī was chosen as a suitable model. In the Tibetan version, the phonological series are ordered as in Devanāgarī (**q.v.**) but the voiced aspirate member of each series is missing: e.g. the velar series is *ka – kha – ga – nga* (minus *gha*). As in Devanāgarī, the short vowel /a/ is inherent in the base consonant. The basic vowels are /i, e, o/, marked by superscript sign, and /u/, marked by subscript.

The accompanying table shows the thirty letters of the consonantal inventory, plus the five additional letters used to denote the retroflex sounds found in Sanskrit words; some examples of conjunct consonants; the vowel signs as applied to the consonant /ka/; the numerals.

The enormous task of translating the Sanskrit/Pali canon into Tibetan began in the eighth century and was not completed until the fourteenth. The Tibetan canon comprises two main divisions: the *Kanjur* (in Tibetan, *bKa'.'gyur* 'word-change', i.e. the Buddha's own words in translation) and the *Tanjur* (in Tibetan, *bsTan.'gyur* 'treatise-change', i.e. the translation of the commentaries). The *Tanjur* alone is in 225 volumes. Part of the translators' task was to provide a lexicon of calques on Sanskrit technical terms, in consistent and one-to-one correspondence with their originals. A measure of the accuracy with which this was accomplished is given by the fact that it is often possible to reconstruct with some certainty Sanskrit originals, which are no longer extant, from their Tibetan calques.

Tibetan spelling, as exemplified in the three proper names given above, requires some explanation. The language is syllabic. Syllables are simple or complex. A simple syllable consists of a consonantal initial (any one of the thirty letters in the basic list) plus a vowel: ꦆ /mi/ 'man'; ꕯ /nga/ 'I'.

A complex syllable has from one to five additional components. These are:

1. The finals: the nine letters ག, ང, ད, ན, བ, མ, འ, ལ, ས function as mute permissible finals. Addition of a final may affect tone and pronunciation: e.g. (initial Roman letters are capitalized here):

   མིག་ [Mig] > /mīī/ 'eye'

   ཆས་ [Čas] > /čɛ̀ɛ̀/ 'clothes'

   ཆོས་ [Čos] > /čȫȫ/ 'dharma, religion'

2. The letters ག, ད, བ, མ, འ, function as mute collinear prefixes, preceding the initial; again, tone and pronunciation are affected: e.g.

   དམག་ [dMag] > /māà/ 'war'

   མདུན་ [mDun] > /tüün/ 'front'

3. The letters ར, ལ, ས are superfixed to the initial; a voiced initial is devoiced:

   སྒོམ་ [sGom] > /qo/ 'meditation'

   སྟབས་ [sTabs] > /tɔ̃p/ 'because'

   ལྷ་ [lHa] > /lhā/ 'god'

4. The letters བ, ཡ, ར, ལ are subfixed to the initial, with secondary forms for ཡ > ◌ྱ and ར > ◌ྲ :

   སྒྲ་ [sGra] > /ṭa/ 'sound'

   ཟློས་ [Zlos] > /ṭȫȫ/ 'chanting, recitation'

5. The letter ས may follow a final (see 1 above):

   ཚོགས་ [TSHogs] > /čɔ̃ɔ̀/ 'assembly'

As an example of a syllable with seven components we may take the perfect stem

 བ་སྒྲུབ་ས [bsGrubs] > /ṭup/ of the stem སྒྲུབ /ṭup/ 'to achieve, acquire'

This syllable comprises a collinear prefix བ་ a superfixed prefix ས, initial ག, subscript ར in secondary form ◌, the vowel /u/ ◌, and two finals, བ and ས་.

The orthography of the words *Kanjur* and *Tanjur* should now be clear:

བཀའ་འགྱུར [bKa'.'Gyur] > /kanjur/

བསྟན་འགྱུར [bsTan.'Gyur] > /tanjur/

(*'gyur* 'to become, be changed'; *bKa'* 'direct word of the Buddha'; *bsTan* – perfect stem of verb *sTon.pa* 'to show, teach').

The retention of the traditional and etymological orthography means that the correspondence between sound and symbol is very weak. For example, *kra, khra, gra, phra, bra, sGra, bsGra* are all ways of writing the phoneme /ṭa/.

It should be pointed out that mute finals may be activated, according to rules of sandhi, in compounds. Thus, while final [g] in [dMag] is mute in citation form, it is activated in e.g. [dMag.cen] > /māqceen/ 'great war'.

THE TIBETAN SCRIPT

CONSONANTS

The *dbu.can* (/u.ceen/) script, consisting of thirty basic letters plus five denoting retroflex sounds in Sanskrit words, is shown here, accompanied by a table of conjunct consonants:

	ka		kya		rju		bla
	kha		kra		lja		rba
	ga		kla		rña		lba
	ṅa		kva		sña		sba
	ca		rka		tra		sbya
	cha		rkya		rta		sbra
	ja		lka		lta		mu
	ña		ska		sta		mya
	ta		skya		thra		mra
	tha		skra		dra		rma
	da		khya		dva		rmya
	na		khra		rda		sma
	pa		khva		lda		smya
	pha		gya		sda		smra
	ba		gra		sdu		tsu
	ma		gla		nra		rtsa
	tsa		gva		rna		rtsva
	tsha		rga		sna		stsa
	dsa		rgya		snra		rdsa
	wa		lga		pu		żu
	ża		sga		pya		zu
	za		sgya		pra		zla
	a, ạ		sgra		lpa		u
	ya		ṅu		spa		yu
	ra						ru
	la						
	śa						

ས	sa	ཾ	rṅa	སྤྱ	spya	ལུ	lu
ཧ	ha	སྙ	sña	སྤྲ	spra	རླ	rla
འ	'a	ལྙ	lña	ཕུ	phu	ཤྲ	śra
ཊ	ṭa	ཅུ	cu	ཕྱ	phya	སུ	su
ཋ	ṭha	ལྕ	lca	ཕྲ	phra	སྲ	sra
ཌ	ḍa	ཆུ	chu	བུ	bu	སླ	sla
ཎ	ṇa	ཇུ	ju	བྱ	bya	ཧྲ	hra
ཥ	ṣa	རྗ	rja	བྲ	bra	ལྷ	lha

The Tibetan vowels i, e, o. shown here as applied to the consonant *ka*:

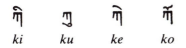

ki   ku   ke   ko

NUMERALS

༡	༢	༣	༤	༥	༦	༧	༨	༩	༠
1	2	3	4	5	6	7	8	9	0

REFERENCES

Beeston, A. F. L. (1937) *Sabean Inscriptions*, Oxford.

Budge, W. (1978) *The Egyptian Language*, Routledge, London

Conti Rossini, C. (1931) *Chrestomathia arabica meridionalis epigraphica*, Rome.

Krjukov, M. V. (1973) *Jazyk In'skix Nadpisej*, Moscow.

Macdonell, A. A. (1924) *Sanskrit Dictionary*, Oxford and London.

Minassian, M. (1976) *Manuel pratique d'arménien ancien*, Paris.

Pfiffig, A. J. (1969) *Die Etruskische Sprache*, Graz.

Sirk, J. X. (1975) *Bugijskij jazyk*, Moscow.